ELYSIAN FIELDS

THE BIRTH OF BASEBALL

THOMAS GILBERT

THE AMERICAN GAME

FRANKLIN WATTS
A Division of Grolier Publishing
New York / London / Hong Kong / Sydney
Danbury, Connecticut

Photographs copyright ©: National Baseball Library and Archive, Cooperstown, N.Y.: pp. 11, 17, 23, 39, 40, 53, 71, 96, 120; Transcendental Graphics: pp. 33, 60, 74, 77, 79, 90, 98, 106, 109, 117.

Library of Congress Cataloging-in-Publication Data

Gilbert, Thomas W.
Elysian Fields : the birth of baseball / by Thomas Gilbert.
p.   cm. — (The American game)
Includes bibliographical references and index.
Summary: Describes the birth and early years of organized baseball, from the first baseball clubs in the 1840s to the activities of the National Association of Professional Base Ball Players in 1871.
ISBN 0-531-11246-2
1. Baseball—United States—History—Juvenile literature.
2. Baseball teams—United States—History—Juvenile literature.
[1. Baseball—History.]   I. Title.   II. Series: The American game.
GV863.G575   1995
357'0973—dc20   95-8935
                                                                     CIP
                                                                      AC

CONTENTS

CHAPTER ONE

A Certain Game of Ball: The New York Game

The small city of Hoboken, New Jersey, lies on the west bank of the Hudson River, a short train ride from New York City's Greenwich Village. If you were to make the trip today to the Hoboken station and then walk north up Hudson Street for a mile or so, you would come to a small green triangle called "Elysian Park" near Hudson Shore Road, Hudson Street, and 10th Street.

There is very little here to suggest that this place was once the bright green expanse, surrounded on three sides by woods, where in June of 1846 eighteen members of a club called the New York Knickerbockers played the very first game of baseball.

To the east the massive Hudson River rushes between New York and New Jersey, bounded on each side by twin no-man's-lands of rotting piers and rusting railroad tracks. An abandoned coffee factory faces the north side of the park, occupying the very spot where some historians locate the infield of that original game. To the west stretches a residential neighborhood made up of blocks of row houses and brownstones.

Only one part of the scenery has remained unchanged in the century and a half since 1846. This is Stevens Castle, which commands a steep hill directly to the south. Once the private home of wealthy industrialist and yachtsman John C. Stevens—the man who won the race that brought yachting's America's Cup to the United States—the castle and much of its former grounds now belong to the Stevens Institute of Technology. Elysian Park itself is barely large enough to contain a few benches, a swing set, and a decrepit metal slide. A sign on a chain-link fence reads, "No Ball Playing."

Who were the New York Knickerbockers, how did they invent baseball, and why did they do it in Hoboken?

To find the answers to these questions, you have to go back through 150 years or so of history, to a time only a few decades after America had fought the two wars that freed it from British domination for good. Fueled by the first stirrings of the industrial revolution, immigration from Europe, and the opening up of the West, America in the 1830s and 1840s was coming into its own geographically, economically, and culturally. Leading the way was New York City, whose economy had been booming ever since the opening of the Erie Canal in 1825.

This was a time before trucks, interstate highways, or extensive railroads. Most goods that had to be shipped overland traveled by barge on canals. By shortening the time it took these goods to go from upstate New York and the Midwest to New York City, the Erie Canal dramatically lowered the cost of basic items like coal and lumber. Overnight, the cost of energy and construction dropped and there was a great building boom. The city expanded in all directions, eventually swallowing up sleepy country villages like Bloomingdale, now part of East Harlem in upper Manhattan, and Bedford, now the inner-city neighborhood of Bedford-Stuyvesant in Brooklyn.

A flood of immigration and economic investment pushed New York ahead of its commercial rivals, Philadelphia and Boston. In the year 1826 five hundred new import-export businesses opened in New York. In the 1830s the waterfronts of Manhattan and Brooklyn constituted the shipbuilding capital of North America, and Manhattan's South Street became the busiest seaport on the East Coast. In 1843, 1,808 ships passed through New York harbor, carrying 45,961 passengers; by 1848 those numbers had leaped to 3,010 ships and 76,671 passengers. Where in 1800 New York's urban sprawl barely extended five blocks north of the present City Hall or about a mile from the southern end of Manhattan Island, by 1850 it had advanced northward nearly all the way to 42nd Street, a distance of almost four miles.

What America did not have in the early nineteenth century was a national sport. But this was about to change. The nation's newfound prosperity led to social changes, many of which directly prepared the way for the birth of the first truly American sport: baseball.

The first change was a new attitude toward leisure and sports. Up to that point in American history, there had been few organized sports and those that did exist, such as yachting and horse racing, were enjoyed almost exclusively by the upper classes. Neither was a likely candidate to become the national sport. Cricket was an exception. It was played by a cross section of Americans, although most of them were immigrants from England and their children. The vast majority of native-born Americans tended to take a Puritanical attitude toward sports and leisure in general. They had inherited the values of the early Pilgrim settlers, which held that sports and games belong to the world of childhood.

To the Puritan way of thinking, for grown men to play or even to watch so-called children's games in public was a scandalous waste of time that could be better spent at something useful, like work or prayer. In the 1830s, for example, a group of Philadelphians began to meet in Camden, New Jersey, to play a primitive bat and ball game called "cat." According to a contemporary account,

> All the players were over 25 years of age, and to see them playing a game like this caused much merriment among the friends of the players. It required "sand" [courage] in those days to go out on the field and play, as the prejudice against the game was very great. It took nearly a whole season to get men enough together to make a team, owing to the ridicule heaped upon the players for taking part in such childish sports.[1]

The increasing industrialization and urbanization of American life in the 1830s and 1840s began to undermine this attitude in two ways. One was a new, stricter division between work time and leisure time. In the eighteenth century, most Americans made a living by farming, by practicing a trade, or by running a small business. Few people worked in offices or factories; their time was their own to divide as they saw fit between work, family, church, and other areas. As the economy of the mid-nineteenth century became more industrial, more and more Americans worked away from home, selling not just their labor but also their time to a boss, company, or office. As more and more workers punched factory clocks or sat at desks through "office hours," the American workday became increasingly distinct from the rest of life.

The flip side of this new organization of work was a new organization of play. After spending long days on the job, people wanted to set aside specific blocks of time to relax and be entertained. A growing number of Americans began to devote occasional afternoons, weekdays, or Sundays to leisure activities. This new leisure movement was led by middle-class and working-class men who had the necessary time and money for such things. In the case of New York City, these men were drawn primarily from three main employment categories: professionals such as lawyers and doctors, lower-level white-collar workers such as bank clerks and shopkeepers, and skilled tradesmen such as butchers, shipwrights, and typesetters. During the 1830s and 1840s, Americans of these classes created an ever-increasing demand for organized fun and games.

The result was the birth of the American entertainment industry. Along New York City's Bowery and in downtown areas of other eastern cities, theater districts sprang up. Show business entrepreneurs built places like Niblo's Garden and the P. T. Barnum Museum in Manhattan, which offered a variety of amusements ranging from spectacles to dramas to musical recitals to industrial fairs to food and drink. For the first time, non-aristocrats in Philadelphia, Boston, and New York began to form racket and other sports clubs. The groundwork was being laid for the phenomenon of organized—and, eventually, spectator—sports.

Another contributing factor to the rise of American sports was a general recognition that life in the crowded American city was becoming unhealthy. In the 1840s, it was fashionable among the wealthy to leave the city and take the "water cure" at rural spas such as Saratoga Springs, New York. In 1850, citing the need for citizens of all classes to enjoy a "healthy atmosphere," New York City set aside the huge parcel of land that would become America's first great urban park, Manhattan's Central Park. The "sedentary habits" of city dwellers were popularly blamed for all sorts of health problems among men, women, and children.

The press took up the cause of athletics as a cure for these problems. For the first time, general newspapers began to publish sports sections and the first magazines and newspapers devoted exclusively to sports, such as the *New York Clipper* and the various incarnations of the *Spirit of the Times*, were founded. One Boston newspaper urged its readers to take up sports because "the tendency toward city life is always towards physical degeneracy, we need something to take us out and away from our killing seclusion and labor." In 1846 the poet and journalist Walt Whitman wrote in the *Brooklyn Eagle*, "In our sun-down perambulations, of late, through the outer parts of Brooklyn, we have observed several parties of youngsters playing 'base,' a certain game of ball. We wish such sights were more common among us; let us go forth awhile, and get better air in our lungs."

Under the influence of ideas like these, the old Puritanical disapproval of sports and exercise began to fade away. Schools introduced physical education into their curricula. Some Protestant churches preached a new, anti-Puritanical doctrine, imported from England, that was called "muscular Christianity." This doctrine taught that physical health could complement spiritual health, instead of acting as a distraction from it. Part of the "muscular Christianity" movement was the Young Men's Christian Association, or YMCA, which crossed the Atlantic from Great Britain in 1851 and energetically promoted baseball and other sports among American young people.

As block after Manhattan block was paved and covered with new buildings, many New Yorkers of the 1840s would escape for a few hours by paying thirteen cents for a round-trip ride on the Barclay Street ferry to the open spaces of Hoboken, New Jersey. There they could breathe fresh country air while strolling through the landscaped grounds of the Elysian Fields, a resort developed by John C. Stevens on property surrounding his riverfront castle and estate. It is no coincidence that Stevens was also the owner of the Barclay Street and other Hudson ferries: one of his purposes in creating the

The famous 1865 match at Elysian Fields between the Atlantics and the Mutuals. The Atlantics won, 13-12.

Elysian Fields was to sell more passenger tickets. At the Elysian Fields, New Yorkers could enjoy the "pleasure railway," a forerunner of the amusement park ride, or have a drink, a smoke, or a meal at McCarty's Hotel or one of many other nearby "reposoires," or taverns. There they could also play bat and ball games—without being laughed at. Stevens's resort hosted spirited cricket matches between the archrival New York Cricket Club and the St. George Cricket Club, a.k.a. the Dragonslayers. In 1845 the Elysian Fields became the home grounds of the New York Knickerbockers baseball club.

Most baseball historians have portrayed the New York Knickerbockers as wealthy aristocrats—men like John C. Stevens. "Let us never forget," writes Albert

Spalding in his 1911 history of baseball, "that the men who first gave impetus to our national sport...were gentlemen 'to the manor born,' men of fine tastes, of high ability, of upright character."

This is pure fantasy. They may have been of high ability and upright character, but the Knickerbockers, like Spalding himself, were decidedly middle class. In a newspaper interview years later, former club president Dr. Daniel Adams recalled his fellow Knickerbockers as consisting primarily of "merchants, lawyers, Union Bank clerks, insurance clerks, and others who were at liberty after three o'clock in the afternoon." According to the club's own membership records, the Knickerbockers also included a manufacturer of barrels, a hatter, a "segar [cigar] dealer," and a United States marshal. Only a handful were wealthy enough to list no occupation next to their name.

Supporting this is the original Knickerbocker constitution of 1845, which refers to players as "gentlemen" and refers to baseball playing as "exercise," implying that the club was engaged in something more serious and more useful than mere play. The Knickerbockers enforced their idea of "gentlemanly" behavior in a decidedly ungentlemanly way, by assessing fines for offenses such as using foul language. They collected so many of these fines that their official scoresheets included a column for "fines," next to those for runs and other game-related statistics.

The tone of the Knickerbockers' code is one of worry that they would be disapproved of or not taken seriously. This kind of anxiety was typically middle class; certainly there would have been nothing less upper class in the 1840s than the Knickerbockers' overriding concern for being seen as respectable. The real American upper classes would hardly have felt it necessary either to proclaim their own gentility or to justify their sports and amusements as "exercise."

The first Knickerbockers came together around 1842 as an informal circle of businessmen and clerks who enjoyed playing bat and ball games, much like the group in Camden and many other East Coast cities. On sunny days, one member would walk down Wall Street in the financial district at lunchtime, rounding up enough players for a pickup game. After the close of bankers' hours in the midafternoon, the players would remove their ties and waistcoats, roll up their sleeves, and carry their homemade bats and crude, rag-stuffed balls to the open spaces north of the city. The Knickerbockers' first playing field was an uneven vacant lot, sparsely covered by grass and weeds, near the intersection of 27th Street and Lexington Avenue in what is now midtown Manhattan. The city's rapid expansion northward soon forced them to relocate farther and farther uptown.

In the beginning, the game they played was not unlike rounders, cat, town ball, or any of the various other baseball-like games played by eighteenth- and nineteenth-century American children. There were few real rules. The number of men on a team, innings in a game, outs in an inning, or strikes and balls in an at-bat varied according to whim. They pitched the ball slowly, put base runners out by hitting them with the ball, and allowed fielders to catch fly balls on one bounce. As in cricket, there was no such thing as foul territory—the ball could be put into play in any direction. They played with a homemade ball that was so light and soft that the outfielders had trouble throwing it to the infield on the fly.

If we could travel back in time and watch the Knicker-bockers playing on a Monday or a Thursday afternoon—their regular play days—in 1842 or 1843, we would recognize their game as a member of the baseball family, but it would seem less like our Major League game than a chaotic cross between whiffleball, inner-city stickball, and suburban Sunday-afternoon beer ball.

Then one day in 1845 an event took place that transformed the Knickerbockers. This was the arrival of a restless entrepreneur named Alexander Joy Cartwright. The son of a ship captain from Nantucket Island in Massachusetts, Cartwright was the kind of ambitious young man that New York City attracted by the thousands in the 1830s and 1840s. Cartwright worked as a clerk at the Union Bank on Wall Street before going in with his brother on a combination bookstore and stationery shop. He was energetic and community-minded: one of Alexander Cartwright's great passions was the volunteer fire department movement.

In those days before cities had professional fire departments, this was an important civic cause. In the first half of the nineteenth century, volunteer fire departments were important social institutions as well. They put on lavish banquets for each other, gave charity balls, and backed political candidates. Beginning in the 1850s, they even fielded baseball teams; the connection with fire companies explains the peculiar names—such as "Alerts," "Red Rovers," and "Resolutes"—of many of the early baseball clubs. Some historians believe that the Knickerbockers took their name from a volunteer fire company to which some of them belonged.

In the spring of 1845 Cartwright convinced his fellow Knickerbockers to form an organized club with formal membership and playing rules and to acquire a regular playing field to solve the problem caused by the rapid disappearance of undeveloped land in Manhattan. As Charles A. Peverelly told the story in his 1866 book *American Pastimes,*

> *During the years of 1842 and '43, a number of gentlemen, fond of the game, casually assembled on a plot of ground in Twenty-Seventh Street...bringing with them their bats, balls, etc.... Among the prominent players were Col. James Lee, Dr. Ransom, Abraham Tucker,*

*James Fisher, W. Vail...[I]n the Spring of 1845
Mr. Alex J. Cartwright...one day upon the field
proposed a regular organization...His proposal
was acceded to, and Messrs. W. R. Wheaton,
Cartwright, D. F. Curry, E. R. Dupignac, Jr., and
W. H. Tucker, formed themselves into a board of
recruiting officers, and soon obtained names
enough to make a respectable show.*[2]

The Knickerbocker officers collected membership dues
and used some of the money to rent a playing field and
dressing room from Stevens's Elysian Fields for seventy-
five dollars a year. For business purposes, they also
rented a boardroom at a Murray Street hotel owned by
one of their members, Charles Fijux. On September 23,
1845, the club's rules committee published a set of
twenty rules. The first rules for baseball that were
intended for use by adults, these twenty rules are the
direct ancestor of the more than one hundred pages of
baseball rules that we play by today.

There are many differing legends about the contributions of Alexander Cartwright. Some say that he was
the first one to come up with the idea of laying the
bases out in a diamond and assigning players to particular
fielding positions. Others say that he is the real author
of the Knickerbockers' first rules. Cartwright's plaque in
the Baseball Hall of Fame at Cooperstown, New York,
credits him with inventing ninety-foot base paths, nine-
man teams, and nine-inning games.

Stripping away the layers of myth and legend from
the story of Alexander Cartwright can be difficult. Some
of these stories may be true; some are clearly false.
What they all have in common, however, is the idea
that Cartwright played a central role in organizing the
Knickerbockers. About this, at least, there can be little
doubt. For one thing, Peverelly directly attributes the
idea of the formal organization of the club to Cartwright.
His account was published only twenty years after the

event, a time when many of the men involved were still living.

Cartwright's descendants in Hawaii and California maintained a separate family tradition that Alexander Cartwright had been the chief inventor of baseball. In 1939 baseball officials resurrected Albert Spalding's 1907 story that Abner Doubleday had invented the game in 1839 in Cooperstown, New York, in order to create a phony "100th anniversary" that coincided with the opening of the National Baseball Hall of Fame. Hearing of this, Cartwright's grandson, Bruce Cartwright, protested to a writer who worked for a national magazine. After the magazine printed excerpts from Alexander Cartwright's diary and other evidence that Cartwright and the Knickerbockers had been the true inventors of baseball, the Hall of Fame compromised by including an "Alexander Cartwright Day" in the opening ceremonies and hanging a portrait of Cartwright in the Hall of Fame alongside that of Doubleday.

Whether written by Cartwright or not, most of the original Knickerbocker baseball rules are very similar to rules for other bat and ball games that appear in children's books from the late eighteenth and early nineteenth centuries. But there are also significant differences that mark the Knickerbocker game as a giant step toward modern baseball. The most important is rule thirteen, which states that a base runner may be forced out or tagged out, but that "in no instance is a ball to be thrown at him." The elimination of this practice, called "soaking" in the nineteenth century and known in various children's games today as "socking" or "Indian rubber," made Knickerbocker baseball a more defensively sophisticated, more dignified game that was much more attractive to adults. Few middle-class businessmen relished a form of "exercise" that included a black eye or bruised ribs. It also allowed the Knickerbockers to develop a harder ball that was more like the ball used in cricket, an English

*Besides inventing baseball, Alexander J. Cartwright,
seen here with fire-fighting gear, founded the
Honolulu, Hawaii, fire department.*

sport with a long tradition of being played by adults. This is the basis for the Knickerbockers' boast that their game was more "manly" than other versions of baseball.

Also in imitation of cricket, the Knickerbocker rules call for the appointment of an umpire to keep statistics in a game book. They set the length of the base paths at somewhere in the neighborhood of the modern ninety feet—the exact distance is debated by historians— established the principle of three outs to an inning, and introduced the idea of pitcher's balks. Probably because their original Manhattan playing fields were continually being crowded, reshaped, and cut off by new streets, buildings, and railroad tracks, the Knickerbockers limited their playing space by introducing the concept of fair and foul territory, an innovation which completely changed the shape of the game.

The language of the twenty rules itself points to the fact that the Knickerbockers' game was a departure from traditional children's bat and ball games. Runs and at-bats, for example, are called "aces" and "hands," terms which were borrowed from adult card games. The influence of card games is also seen in rule eight, which defines the winner not as the team with the most runs after nine innings, but as the first team to reach twenty-one runs after an equal number of innings had been played.

We know from the Knickerbockers' original game book, which survives today as part of the New York Public Library's Spalding Collection, that the Knicker- bockers experimented with these new rules throughout the fall of 1845 and the spring of 1846. A note in the game book also tells us that the club's first "match game," meaning the first formal contest with another club, took place on the afternoon of Thursday, June 19, 1846. The Knickerbockers' opponent that day is identi- fied as the "New York Nine."

It is not clear exactly who the New York Nine were. They may have been cricketers. They may have been a pickup team made up of some outsiders and some Knickerbockers; some of the names in the New York lineup are identified in other lineups as Knickerbockers. There is also sketchy evidence that they may have been members of an older, unorganized baseball club, some of whose younger members broke away to form the Knickerbockers.

Either way, they were certainly not beginners. In the game that the Knickerbockers themselves considered their first formal match, the inventors of modern baseball were destroyed by the New York Nine 23-1 in four innings. The New York Nine's only setback was a six-cent fine assessed by the unnamed umpire on leadoff man Davis for "swearing." Thanks to the Knickerbocker game book, we also have the following box score for the game of June 19:

KNICKERBOCKER			NEW YORK		
	O.	R.		O.	R.
Turney	1	0	Davis	1	3
Adams	1	0	Winslow	2	2
Tucker	2	0	Ransom	2	3
Birney	1	1	Murphy	0	4
Avery	0	0	Case	0	4
H. Anthony	2	0	Johnson	1	2
D. Anthony	2	0	Thompson	2	2
Tryon	2	0	Trenchard	2	1
Paulding	1	0	Lalor	2	2
	12	1		12	23

This primitive box score does not look like the beginning of anything as important as modern baseball. It contains only the names of the players and two statistical categories: outs—also called "hands lost"—and runs. It does not tell us much about how the game went. And only in a very narrow sense can it be called a record of the first baseball game; Americans had been hitting a ball and running bases since the arrival of the first English colonists. They had been playing games resembling baseball and even games that were called baseball for generations before the Knickerbockers met the New York Nine. The journal of one Revolutionary War soldier mentions that George Washington's troops relieved the winter boredom of Valley Forge by playing "base."

The real significance of the Knickerbockers' first game has to do not with who the players were or what the score was, but with what came after it. By organizing the first baseball club and publishing the first sophisticated baseball rules for adults, Alexander Cartwright and the Knickerbockers provided a model for other men's clubs to follow and separated organized baseball forever from the world of childhood play. In the late 1800s these men's clubs united to form the National Association of Base Ball Players (NABBP). In 1871 the NABBP gave way to the National Association, the first professional league, which was replaced in 1876 by the present National League. All of today's baseball organizations—from sandlot, high school, and college leagues to the professional minors and majors—can be traced back to Alexander Cartwright and the Knickerbockers. Without these baseball pioneers, we would have had no Giants-Dodgers rivalry or World Series seventh games; no Wrigley Field, Fenway Park, or Toronto Skydome; no Charlie Finley, Marvin Miller, or Kenesaw Mountain Landis; no Babe Ruth, Joe DiMaggio, or Jackie Robinson; no Mickey Mantle, Josh Gibson, Nolan Ryan, Roberto Clemente, or Ken Griffey, Jr. On June 19, 1846, baseball took the first step on its long journey from a casual pastime to the national sport and multibillion-dollar entertainment business that it has become today.

CHAPTER TWO

Abner Doubleday: The Man Who Did Not Invent Baseball

Baseball has an alternative explanation for its origins, one that has nothing to do with Alexander Cartwright or the New York Knickerbockers: the Abner Doubleday story.

The Abner Doubleday story goes like this: In 1839 Abner Doubleday, a nineteen-year-old studying at Green's Select School in Cooperstown, New York, invented a new game and taught it to a group of friends who played bat and ball games in a field belonging to a farmer named Phinney. He called the game "base ball." By himself, he came up with the idea of laying out the bases in a diamond, the idea of assigning players to set positions, and much of the rest of the basic structure of the game.

There is just one problem with the Abner Doubleday tale: It is not true. Abner Doubleday had an interesting and varied life. He was a writer, an engineer, a surveyor, and an army general, who, at Fort Sumter, South Carolina, aimed the first cannon fired by the Union in the Civil War; he later distinguished himself at the Battle of Gettysburg. After his retirement from military service,

Doubleday traveled to San Francisco to build the first cable car system in the United States. But Doubleday did not go to school in Cooperstown; he was a cadet at West Point military academy during the years 1839 and 1840.

Doubleday was born in Ballston Spa, New York, sixty miles from Cooperstown, but there is no record that he ever set foot in Cooperstown either before or after 1839. Even though he was a widely published writer and a voluminous diarist, Abner Doubleday left behind no evidence that he had any connection at all with baseball, even as a casual fan. Doubleday once described his boyhood as follows: "I was fond of poetry and art and mathematical studies. In my outdoor sports I was addicted to topographical work, and even as a boy amused myself by making maps of the country."[1] If any of the speakers at Doubleday's grand 1893 New York City funeral had suggested that the late general had been the inventor of America's national pastime, the reaction surely would have been complete and utter astonishment.

The Abner Doubleday story is so ridiculous that it is not really worth "debunking." The more interesting point about it is the question of who created it out of whole cloth and why. That story begins at an 1889 dinner given at Delmonico's restaurant in New York City to celebrate the completion of Albert Spalding's around-the-world baseball tour. A former star pitcher in the National League, Spalding was the millionaire owner of the Chicago White Stockings—who, in spite of their name, were the ancestor not of the Chicago White Sox, but of today's Chicago Cubs—and the Spalding sporting goods empire. Designed to spread the gospel of baseball—and to promote Spalding's sporting goods—throughout the world, the tour consisted of a series of exhibition games played across the Pacific, Asia, North Africa, and Europe by teams made up of major leaguers.

Spalding's tour was a mixed success. The Americans were a big hit in Australia, drawing crowds of ten thou-

22

Civil War hero Abner Doubleday in military uniform

sand and inspiring predictions by local sportswriters that baseball would soon become popular there. (They turned out to be right; today Australia has a thriving baseball scene and has produced catcher Dave Nilsson, shortstop Craig Shipley, and several other players who have made it to the American big leagues.) On the other hand, during visits to Sri Lanka and elsewhere in Asia they were stared at, according to one of the players, as though they were "so many escaped inmates." Arriving in Europe, Spalding played the ugly American, offending Italians by asking the pope to pose for a team picture and offering five thousand dollars to rent the Colosseum for a game. The Americans were politely received by the English public, even though Spalding committed the terrible gaffe of publicly grabbing the Prince of Wales's shoulder during a game at Kensington Oval cricket grounds in London.

The English stop on the tour was further marred for Spalding by the insistence of many members of the cricket establishment that American baseball was nothing more than a new name for an old English bat and ball game called "rounders." This is certainly an exaggeration; baseball is far more complex than rounders and there are many significant differences between the two games. But there are similarities as well; rounders is nearly identical to town ball, an American precursor of baseball. The idea that baseball is a form of rounders or that it came from rounders makes a lot more sense than, say, the Doubleday myth. But to Spalding, National League President A. G. Mills, and the other American players and executives who had accompanied him to England, the comparison was a terrible put-down. This is because rounders was (and still is, in England and in many former British colonies) a game for girls and young children.

As they sat down weeks later to their Delmonico's steak dinners and listened to the featured speaker, Mark Twain, praise baseball as the "very symbol, the outward and visible expression of the drive and push and rush and struggle of the raging, tearing, booming nineteenth century," Spalding and the rest of the American baseball tourists were still angry. When the time came for A. G. Mills to speak, he addressed the rounders question. "Patriotism and research," he announced, "had proven that baseball was not derived from rounders, cricket, or any other English game." Baseball, he said over enthusiastic shouts of "no rounders, no rounders!" from the audience, owed nothing to any foreign influence. It was, in the phrase of the New York Giants shortstop John Montgomery Ward, entirely the product of the "genius of the American boy."

The rounders controversy lasted for years after the Delmonico's dinner, driven primarily by two forces. One was lingering injured American pride over what Spalding called "the sneering comments" about baseball made by the English. The other was the writings of English-born journalist Henry Chadwick, who rankled Spalding by arguing in his best-selling baseball books and annual guides that baseball had grown out of rounders. Chadwick was a lifelong promoter of baseball who, while serving on various national baseball rules committees, had played a key role in the evolution of baseball's rules. Because he was widely respected in the nineteenth century as the "father of baseball," his opinions carried great weight.

Throughout the early 1900s, Chadwick and Spalding carried on the rounders debate, although neither of them seems to have taken it entirely seriously. When you really look at it, the area of disagreement between the two was actually very small. Unlike some of the snobbish cricketers Spalding had encountered on his world tour, Chadwick meant no disrespect to baseball by comparing it to rounders. As he put it in his 1868 book, *The Game of Baseball,* "From this little English acorn of Rounders has the giant American oak of Base Ball grown, and just as much difference exists between the British schoolboy sport and our American national game, as between the seedling and the full grown king of the forest."[2]

This was far from a controversial statement when it was published. In 1878 Spalding himself had written in his own annual baseball guide that baseball "unquestionably originated" from rounders. It was only after the 1888–89 world tour that he declared: "I have been fed on this kind of 'Rounders pap' for upwards of forty years, and I refuse to swallow any more of it without substantial proof sauce of it." Further evidence of the lightheartedness of the great rounders debate is the fact that Chadwick and Spalding remained the closest of friends. Chadwick later dismissed the whole thing as a "joke between Albert and myself."

In 1905 Spalding may have carried the joke too far. That year he appointed a blue-ribbon commission, chaired by his close friend A. G. Mills and including two United States senators, to settle the question of baseball's origins "in some comprehensive and authoritative way, and for all time." Two years later the Mills commission issued a report that introduced the Doubleday story to the world. The report concluded: "First— that baseball had its origin in the United States; Second— that the first scheme for playing it, according to evidence obtainable to date, was devised by Abner Doubleday, at Cooperstown, New York, in 1839." As evidence for this proposition the Mills commission offered nothing more than a single letter from a mining engineer named Abner Graves. Graves, who later was hospitalized for mental illness, claimed to have been present at farmer Phinney's field in Cooperstown the day Doubleday presented his idea for the first baseball diamond. The Mills commission offered nothing to back this up. Its report includes no personal testimony from its own chairman, who besides serving as a baseball executive had been a lifelong friend of Doubleday. Presumably, if Abner Doubleday really had invented baseball, he might have mentioned that fact to his good friend A. G. Mills, the baseball man.

As history, the Graves letter is absurd. But it served the Mills commission's propaganda purpose perfectly by providing a specific and all-American origin for baseball. And there was an added benefit: By associating America's national sport with the Union victory in the Civil War through the war hero General Abner Doubleday, the commission wrapped baseball in the Stars and Stripes. Spalding's first comments on the Mills Commission report spell this out very plainly. "It certainly appeals to an American's pride," he said, "to have had the great national game of Base Ball created and named by a Major General in the United States Army." After the Mills report came out, anyone who suggested that baseball had come from the English game of rounders ran the risk of being called unpatriotic.

Spalding popularized the Doubleday myth by publishing it with a straight face in his widely read 1911 history, *Baseball: America's National Game*. It was revived in 1939 in order to justify the building of the National Baseball Hall of Fame in Cooperstown, just down the street from the site of farmer Phinney's field. Since then, it has been repeated by countless broadcasters, sportswriters, and historians. But none of this explains how Albert Spalding's fairy tale has been able to keep its grip on the American imagination for almost ninety years without having the slightest basis in fact.

The truth is that, crudely designed as it was to appeal to the chauvinism of our great-grandparents, the Doubleday story has endured precisely because of its unreality. A rosy and nostalgic tale situated far from the crowded, smoky cities where baseball really was born, this version of baseball's creation contains no lawyers, bank clerks, or rules committees. By locating the game's beginnings in the country and crediting its invention to a teenager, the Abner Doubleday story satisfies a sentimental longing—that is almost as old as baseball itself—of Americans to root the often hard-boiled business of baseball in innocent childhood play and in the nation's small-town rural past.

CHAPTER
THREE

Playing for the Fun of It:
The Knickerbocker Era

Baseball went through more changes in the fifteen years between the first game played by the Knicker-bockers and the outbreak of the Civil War than it has in the entire twentieth century. It began in 1846 as a way for a few dozen New York clerks to loosen their limbs after long hours spent sitting behind their desks. There were no baseball uniforms, box scores, batting averages, or pennant races; the game itself was virtually unheard of outside of lower Manhattan and nearby Hoboken, New Jersey.

By 1860, however, baseball Knickerbocker-style was being played by Americans everywhere—from boys and girls in playgrounds and schoolyards to youngsters in amateur leagues to accomplished adult athletes playing before large crowds of paying fans. Even before Abner Doubleday fired his cannon at Fort Sumter, referring to baseball as the "national pastime" was already a cliché.

Before it won over America, however, the Knicker-bockers' game first had to conquer New York. During the 1850s the New York City metropolitan area became a laboratory where baseball experimented with new rules, playing techniques, and organizational structures. This process began when hundreds of middle-class men in New York City, most of them working in the financial district or in other white-collar jobs, saw Alexander Cartwright's exciting new game and caught baseball fever. Several new baseball clubs sprang up, using the Knickerbockers and their twenty rules as a model. By the middle 1850s baseball was popular enough across neighborhood and class lines that box scores and game reports began to appear regularly in newspaper sports sections.

Cartwright himself did not stick around long enough to see his game become the favorite pastime of New York stockbrokers and bank clerks. In January of 1848 gold was discovered at Sutter's Mill near Sacramento, California. The following year tens of thousands of ambitious young men from all over the United States, among them the writers Mark Twain, Bret Harte, and Ambrose Bierce, crossed the unsettled Great Plains and headed for the gold fields of California. In the spring of 1849 the twenty-nine-year-old Alexander Cartwright and a dozen friends joined the mad rush westward.

Like most of his fellow "Forty-Niners," Cartwright did not achieve his dream of easy money. In those days, the journey to California was brutally difficult. It took Cartwright and his party most of a summer to trek overland by horse, foot, and wagon train all the way to San Francisco from the end of the rail line at Pittsburgh. After living for months on nothing but buffalo meat and fighting off attacks by fierce Plains Indians, Cartwright arrived in California homesick and completely cured of gold fever. He bought a ticket on a ship bound for New York via the Pacific Ocean and China. But travel by sea agreed with him even less than travel by land. Near the Sandwich Islands, now known as Hawaii, Cartwright came down with a horrific case of seasickness and was put ashore at Honolulu. There he decided to give up traveling for good and sent for his wife and children.

Alexander Cartwright never sailed again. He spent the rest of his life in Hawaii, dying in 1892 as one of the islands' leading citizens. Besides having founded one of the islands' first and most successful banks, the enterprising Cartwright had served as financial adviser to the Hawaiian royal family, consul for the government of Peru, and chairman of the Honolulu Chamber of Commerce.

Cartwright may have left New York and the Knickerbockers, but he took with him his twin enthusiasms for baseball and volunteer firefighting. He founded Honolulu's first fire department and served for many years as its director. He eagerly taught the New York game of baseball to anyone he met along his journey to the West. Because of Cartwright, baseball Knickerbocker-style was known on the western frontier before it was played in Chicago, Boston or Baltimore. Certainly it took root in Hawaii before it had even been heard of in most mainland states.

Cartwright kept a diary of his trip which survives today in fragments. One entry reads: "April 23, 1849. During the past week we have passed the time fixing wagon covers, stowing property, etc., varied by hunting, fishing and playing baseball. It is comical to see the mountain men and Indians playing the new game. I have the ball with me we used back home."[1] Throughout his time in Hawaii, Cartwright visited local schools to teach the fundamentals of baseball both to Hawaiian children and to the children of mainlanders.

With or without Alexander Cartwright, the Knickerbockers dominated the New York baseball scene. The other baseball clubs copied the stylish blue and white uniforms—probably inspired by those worn by contemporary firemen—that were adopted by the Knickerbockers in 1849. Remnants of the old New York Nine formed the Washington Club and then reformed as the Gothams. Both clubs played their home games at the

Red House, a country inn in then-rural Harlem in upper Manhattan. A friendly rivalry sprang up as the Gothams and Knickerbockers crisscrossed the Hudson River to play a best-two-out-of-three, home-and-home series at the Red House and the Elysian Fields.

These matches stirred up tremendous interest. The *New York Herald* and the *Sunday Mercury*, another New York newspaper, began to print accounts of this new, all-American sport next to reports of cricket matches and other more traditional sporting events. On July 10, 1853, the *Mercury* noted, "The Gotham and Knickerbocker clubs played a match game, on the grounds of the latter, at Hoboken, on the 5th inst. The Knickerbockers won. Gotham, 18 outs, 12 runs; Knickerbockers, 18 outs, 21 runs."[2] The Knickerbockers took the series 2-0 by defeating the Gothams at home on October 14 by a score of 21-14.

Baseball has always been driven by great rivalries. In our century we have the Dodgers-Giant rivalry and the Yankees-Red Sox rivalry. In the 1850s, many of the fans who had been caught up in the excitement of the Knickerbocker-Gotham series formed their own clubs. By 1854 there were dozens of baseball clubs around the New York metropolitan area, but a select four were recognized as the elite: the Knickerbockers, the Gothams, the Eagles, and the Empires. All of these clubs were based in Manhattan. All played most of their games at the Elysian Fields, used the official rules published annually by the Knickerbocker club, and emulated the Knickerbockers' club constitution and overall style. A few lines from the team song of one early club show the respected position occupied by the Knickerbockers in the small baseball world of that time:

> *And should any club by their cunning and trick*
> *Dishonor the game that it plays;*
> *Let them take my advice and go to "Old Knick,"*
> *And there learn to better their ways.*[3]

31

As much as they looked up to "Old Knick" as a model of sportsmanship, however, it was not long before these new clubs caught up with or even surpassed the Knickerbockers on the baseball diamond. With more and better athletes playing baseball each season, the level of competition inevitably rose and any advantage the Knickerbockers enjoyed by having played baseball first soon evaporated. One indication of the general improvement in fielding techniques and in defensive teamwork is the fact that it took teams more and more innings to score the 21 runs required for a victory. (Imagine how long games would last today, if we played to 21 runs.)

In the opening game of the 1854 series between the Knickerbockers and Gothams, the Gothams took an unprecedented three hours to win 21-16 in sixteen innings. The Knickerbockers took the second game at the Elysian Fields 24-13 in nine innings. One newspaper described the rubber match as follows: "One of the most exciting and interesting games ever played was the closing one for 1854 at the Red House, Harlem, occupying two hours, with 12 runs each in 12 innings, which could not be concluded for want of daylight."[4] By 1855, the Gothams had surpassed the Knickerbockers as the best baseball club. The following year the Knickerbockers dropped to fourth place among the elite clubs.

What was baseball like in the Knickerbocker era? From the records kept by the early clubs themselves and from New York City newspapers, which began to give baseball more coverage as the 1850s went on, we can get a fairly complete picture of how the game played by the Knickerbockers, Empires, Gothams, and Eagles compares to the game that we play today.

Some of the greatest differences were off the field. Baseball clubs of the 1850s, for example, were really clubs. Unlike today's professional baseball clubs, which are profit-making corporations made up of workers,

*The New York Knickerbockers and the
Brooklyn Excelsiors before a game in 1858.
The figure in the top hat and dark coat is umpire
and Excelsiors president Dr. J. B. Jones.*

managers, and investors, the Knickerbockers and their competitors were more like modern country clubs or racquet clubs. They were strictly amateur: No one in the 1850s made a living by playing baseball and no fan had to buy a ticket in order to see a game. This meant that the players themselves ran their own clubs and contributed the money for their support. There were no owners, general managers, managers, or scouts. Amateur clubs divided their players by playing ability into separate teams: there would be a "first nine," a "second nine," and so on, down to the "amateur" and "muffin" nines at the bottom. Clubs recruited their own players and teams were led on the field by playing captains elected by their teammates.

Like many of our present-day country clubs, the Knickerbockers and the other early baseball clubs were more than just athletic organizations. They were concerned about social status. Besides enforcing codes of behavior through monetary fines, they asserted their respectability by excluding people they considered beneath them socially. Any club member could anonymously "blackball," or block the admission of, a prospective member for any reason. The effect of this was that the first baseball clubs were made up exclusively of friends and social equals of the Knickerbockers. It also meant that, like most contemporary middle-class institutions in the North, they were all-white. No African American or player from the semiskilled or unskilled working classes need apply.

The baseball clubs of the 1850s devoted at least as much energy to socializing as to sports. The baseball season lasted only five or six months, but baseball clubs put on dances, charity balls, and dinners for players, their families, and guests throughout the year. In this they resembled not only our modern country clubs, but also nineteenth-century volunteer fire companies, which were famous for their chowder suppers and other civic functions. A New York newspaper described an 1854 joint baseball dinner for the Knickerbockers, Eagles, and Gothams as follows:

> *An equal delegation was present, and an excellent bill of fare presented. The utmost hilarity prevailed, and everything passed off in a happy manner. A song, composed for the occasion by James Whyte Davis of the Knickerbocker Club, was so well received that the Eagle Club had it printed. It was entitled "Ball Days" and abounded in witty allusions to the principal players of the three clubs.*[5]

Because there were no leagues or schedules, matches came about when a baseball club issued a challenge to a rival in the form of a written invitation for the clubs to meet on a particular date. Again, this may have been inspired by the volunteer fire companies' practice of challenging rival companies to races and water-pumping contests. For both fire companies and baseball clubs, it was the custom of the challenger to offer lavish post-contest entertainments. These would include a sumptuous formal dinner, often all-male, followed by rounds of toasting and treats such as ice cream, brandy, and cigars. Baseball club dinners also frequently featured musical bands and speech making. Compare the following newspaper item from 1858 to a modern game story:

> *On the 20th of August, the return match was played...at Elysian Fields, which was one of the finest games ever played; the score standing, at the end of nine innings, 15 to 14, in favor of the Excelsiors. At the close of this match, the Excelsior Club was escorted to Odd Fellow's Hall, Hoboken, by the Knickerbocker Club, and entertained in splendid style, covers being laid for over 200 gentlemen. Dodsworth's Band [one of the first blackface, or minstrel, acts] was in attendance to enliven the scene, and all the arrangements were exceedingly creditable to the taste and liberality of the committee who had charge of the festive occasion.*[6]

Reading newspaper sports sections from the 1850s, you sometimes expect to see a menu at the bottom of a baseball story instead of a box score.

As for how the game of the 1850s was played, if we could somehow travel through time and go to a match between the Knickerbockers and the Gothams, we would find most aspects of the game to be pretty familiar. Although not specified in the Knickerbockers' original 1846 rules, it had now become customary to play nine men to a side. The bases may have been made out of iron (painted white), but they were laid out in a diamond pattern roughly similar to a modern infield. With the exception of the shortstop, who served as a roving universal cut-off man on throws from the outfield, players played nearly the same defensive positions as in today's game.

A few things about 1850s baseball, however, would strike a visitor from the twentieth century as very odd. The first would be the complete absence of gloves; fielders had to play batted balls bare-handed and as a result, suffered many bruises, smashed fingers, and split lips. The second would be the sad predicament of the pitcher.

In today's game, the pitcher is the most important player on the field. More often than not, how he plays determines whether his team wins or loses. Under the Knickerbocker rules, however, the pitcher was by far the least important player. The pitcher of the 1840s and 1850s stood only forty-five feet from home plate, but according to the rules he had to "pitch" (that is, toss underhand) rather than "throw" (meaning throw overhand), the baseball to the batters with an easy motion. With men on base, he was at a terrible disadvantage; he could not throw the ball too fast, or the gloveless catcher would not be able to stop it. Curve balls were out of the question, because pitchers were not allowed to snap their wrists or bend their pitching elbows. Change-ups, knuckleballs, forkballs, and the rest of the trick pitches in the repertoire of the modern pitcher would have been equally useless. This is because no strikes or balls were called by the umpire; the batter could simply wait until he got a perfect pitch to swing at. Not surprisingly, there were a lot of runs in 1850s baseball. Scores in double figures were the rule and most games saw 50, 60, or even 70 or 80 runs scored. For the season of 1857 the lowest-scoring game on record was the Atlantics' 19-3 victory over the Putnams.

Baseball in the Knickerbocker era was a genteel affair. True to the spirit of Alexander Cartwright and baseball's other founding fathers, members of the Gotham, Eagle, Empire, and Knickerbocker clubs in the early and middle 1850s kept the game to themselves and to fellow members of the respectable middle classes. For them, baseball was still an "exercise"—not an all-out struggle to win. They subordinated their natural human competitiveness with elaborate rituals and displays of sportsmanship. The baseball clubs of the Knickerbocker era really believed that it was not whether you won or lost that mattered, but how you played the game.

These values lasted as long as "Old Knick" dictated to the rest of the clubs on matters of playing rules, club organization, and playing philosophy. Before the end of the 1850s, however, the world of the Knickerbockers was becoming a victim of its own success. Increasing popularity led to a breakdown of Knickerbocker values and baseball lost much of its gentility. Clubs began to concentrate more on winning games and less on hosting fancy banquets. Invitations for matches began to specify, "No collation [postgame dinner] will be given." In 1859 postgame banquets were officially discouraged by the National Association of Base Ball Players, baseball's national governing body, as a distraction from competition on the field. Players practiced hard to develop their hitting skills. Fielders experimented with new techniques. No longer content to serve as human batting tees, pitchers bent the Knickerbocker pitching rules further and further in order to get hitters out with deceptive motions and changes of speed.

As baseball evolved and spread, the high ideals of amateurism and sportsmanship that the Knickerbockers stood for began to seem old-fashioned. In 1855 the Knickerbockers were outraged when the Gothams borrowed a "ringer," or star player, from the Unions of Morrisania (now part of the Bronx in New York City) for one of their match games. During the off-season, the Knickerbockers tried—and failed—to eliminate this practice by passing a rule against it. Baseball was slipping out of the Knickerbockers' control.

Part of the problem was geographical; baseball was no longer confined to a few hundred residents of lower Manhattan Island. In 1854 a group of young Brooklynites, returning from a match at the Elysian Fields between the Knickerbockers and the Eagles, decided to form the first baseball club on the Brooklyn bank of the East River. (Brooklyn was then an independent city; it did not become part of New York City until 1898.) They gave it the awkward name "Jolly Young Bachelors Base Ball Club," which was soon changed to the "Excelsiors." Proclaiming themselves the "Knickerbockers of Brooklyn," they played their games in what is now South Brooklyn; their elegant brick and wrought iron clubhouse still stands on Clinton Street in Brooklyn Heights.

In 1855 the Excelsiors were joined on the Brooklyn baseball scene by the Putnams, the Atlantics, and the Eckfords. The Eckfords were unusual in that they were made up of shipwrights from Greenpoint, now a neighborhood in North Brooklyn. All were employed by the Scottish shipbuilder Henry Eckford—yet another New Yorker with connections both to baseball and to volunteer firefighting. Eckford sponsored a famous fire company that was nicknamed "Old Turk" after Eckford took several of its members to Istanbul, Turkey, on a construction job.

Historians often cite the Eckfords as proof that baseball fever had begun to infect the lower classes, but this is exaggerated. The job of shipwright may not have been white-collar, but in the New York of the 1850s it was roughly comparable in respectability and status to the low-level Wall Street jobs held by Alexander Cartwright and his friends. The Eckfords were far from working-class in the modern sense. This was no group of

*The Brooklyn Excelsiors baseball club in 1859;
the great Jim Creighton stands third from the left.*

Archie Bunkers—not only did they put on fancy dinners and dress balls that equaled those of the Knickerbockers and Gothams; they even fielded a cricket team.

The real significance of the Eckfords and the other new baseball clubs that sprang up like mushrooms all over the Bronx, Queens, New Jersey, and Long Island in the middle and late 1850s is not that the game was being taken over by the working classes, but simply that baseball had entered the urban mainstream in all of its variety. In 1856, 1857, and 1858, dozens and dozens of new baseball clubs were formed around the metropolitan area by all kinds of people.

Numerous fire companies fielded baseball teams, among them the Mutual Hook and Ladder Company,

The crooked New York Mutuals of the early 1870s

which became the personal club of New York mayor and Tammany Hall leader Boss Tweed. The Mutuals would become a national baseball power in the 1870s and a charter member of the National Association, the first baseball major league. Guilds and trade associations formed teams with names like Typographical, Chestnut Street Theatre, and Fulton Market; doctors formed the Aesculapian club and bartenders formed a team called the Phantoms. Neighborhood teams like the Putnams, Harlems, and Bedfords took the names of streets or communities. Patriotic names were most common, among them Washington, Jefferson, Hamilton, Franklin, and Liberty.

Baseball crossed age as well as geographical and social lines, as junior clubs like Young America, Star, and Enterprise were formed by young men and boys. According to historian Harold Seymour, in 1858 there were approximately fifty adult clubs and sixty or more junior clubs in the vicinity of New York City and Brooklyn. One New York City newspaper stated in 1856 that baseball was being played on every open acre within ten miles of the city limits.

By 1856 even the Knickerbockers recognized that baseball needed some kind of organizational structure. For a decade baseball's only authority had been the executive committee of the Knickerbocker Base Ball Club. All baseball questions were settled at the annual meetings of the Knickerbockers. The other baseball clubs were not represented at these meetings; their only choice was to follow the Knickerbockers in all things.

The tremendous popularity explosion of the middle 1850s made it necessary to establish a broader governing body that would give a voice to the other baseball clubs. In December 1856, after a motion by James Whyte Davis (the author of the baseball song that was so well received at the Knickerbocker-Eagle-Gotham baseball dinner of 1854), Knickerbockers president Dr. Daniel Adams issued an invitation for the principal New York-area clubs to meet at a "general baseball convention" the following May to agree on common rules and other issues. Attending the 1857 convention were delegates from the following clubs: Knickerbocker, Gotham, Eagle, Empire, Eckford, Union, Atlantic, Excelsior, Harlem, Continental, Nassau, Baltic, Bedford, Harmony, and Olympic. All of these were based in New York City, in Brooklyn, or in outlying towns that were later absorbed by the present boroughs of Brooklyn and Queens. The convention approved a new code of rules, including the provision that nine innings would now constitute a game.

A second baseball convention, this time with delegates representing twenty-six clubs, was held in 1858. This convention created a national umbrella organization, named the National Association of Base Ball Players (NABBP), which was to hold annual baseball conventions in New York City. The association included a board of elected officers and a separate three-man rules committee. The NABBP continued to hold ever-larger annual conventions into the 1870s, when it gave way to the organized leagues that are the direct ancestors of today's professional and amateur leagues.

If the baseball conventions of the late 1850s marked the beginning of a new democracy in baseball, they also signaled the final decline of Knickerbocker influence. The convention of 1856 was called by Knickerbockers president Dr. Daniel Adams at the suggestion of a fellow Knickerbocker; Adams also presided over the convention of 1857. In 1858, however, the new association elected its own slate of officers. They were W. H. Van Cott of the Gothams, president; J. B. Jones of the Excelsiors, vice president; Thomas S. Dakin of the (Brooklyn) Putnams, second vice president; J. Ross Postley of the Metropolitans, recording secretary; Theodore F. Jackson of the Putnams, corresponding secretary; and E. H. Brown of the Metropolitans, treasurer. Significantly, there is not a single Knickerbocker on the list. While Adams continued to serve on the NABBP rules committee, neither he nor any other Knickerbocker was ever again elected to a major baseball office.

Over the next two decades the Knickerbockers faded from the national baseball scene. Disdaining the increasing competitiveness and professionalism of the sport that they had pioneered, the Knickerbockers played pickup games among themselves, or with a few of the older clubs, by their own rules and customs. One of those customs was strict amateurism. They refused to play for a share of the gate, a practice that became common after clubs began to charge admission to baseball grounds in the 1860s. James Whyte Davis, one of the oldest Knickerbockers, resigned his membership when other club members agreed to play in a game to which admission was charged—even though it had been specified that the Knickerbockers would not get a penny of the money. Scheduling fewer and fewer matches with other clubs and refusing to join any league, they continued to play baseball—as Cartwright and his friends had originally intended—for exercise and for fun. As one reporter wrote in 1863, describing a lopsided defeat of the Knickerbockers by the far more skillful Excelsiors, "The Knickerbockers play ball because they love it. They turn out for sport simply, and have plenty of it."

Thanks to the New York Knickerbockers, baseball had come a long way in the 1840s and 1850s. In an 1896 newspaper interview, Dr. Adams remembered that in the early days the clubs' biggest problem was getting enough players to show up to make two teams. By the 1860s, Adams continued, "thousands were present to witness matches, and any number of outside players [stood] ready to take a hand on regular playing days. We pioneers never expected to see the game so universal as it has now become."[7] But the national baseball conventions of 1856, 1857, and 1858 made it clear that baseball would be making the rest of its journey without Alexander Cartwright's club. The Knickerbocker era was over.

National Pastimes: Town Ball and the New England Game

The twenty-six clubs who in 1858 called themselves the National Association of Base Ball Players, were being a little loose with words. Not only was the organization not national—nearly all of its members came from New York—it would have been an exaggeration even to call it the *New York State* Association of Base Ball Players. None of its members was located more than a few miles outside the city limits of New York City or Brooklyn.

There was another problem with the NABBP: The New York game, as Knickerbocker-style baseball was then known, was not the only type of baseball being played by American adults in the 1850s. The same social and economic changes that made it possible for Alexander Cartwright and the Knickerbockers to transform baseball from a children's pastime into a serious adult sport had also taken place in other American cities, mainly in New York's chief commercial and cultural rivals, Boston and Philadelphia.

Baseball developed in these three cities in a remarkably parallel way. At about the same time that the Knickerbockers developed baseball in New York, Bostonians invented the "Massachusetts" or "New England" game and Philadelphians came up with their own variety of baseball called "town ball." The Knickerbockers were more highly organized and were the first to print formal rules, but all three cities had their own baseball clubs and associations by the early 1850s. These different brands of baseball continued to evolve independently through the late 1850s. Eventually, the three games came into contact with each other and a rivalry sprang up over which one would become the true national game. As late as the year 1857, it was not clear which type of baseball would win out. By the time of the Civil War, however, the New York game had won a decisive victory and the others were quickly forgotten. Today, it is a rare fan, even in Boston or Philadelphia, who has even heard of town ball or the New England game.

The Philadelphia game grew out of town ball, an American version of rounders which was played informally all over the United States even before the Revolutionary War. The name came from the fact that it was played on holidays, when farmers would go to the nearest town for a celebration, or on town meeting days. The first Philadelphia town ball club came out of that tradition; it began by playing only once a year, as a way to celebrate the Fourth of July. It first became organized in 1831 when, just as the original Knickerbockers had crossed the Hudson, a group of Philadelphians crossed the Delaware River to Camden, New Jersey, in search of an open field to play ball. In 1833 this group merged with another that played on Market Street in the city to form the Olympic Ball Club.

Like the Knickerbockers, the Olympics had a formal constitution and rules. The Olympics seem to have been a more aristocratic group than the Knickerbockers. Many of them went to school together and their name suggests an educational connection; the basis of nineteenth-century high school and college education was the study of the classics, or the Greek and Roman languages, culture, and history. The Olympic Games were the national sporting festival of the ancient Greeks.

Like their New York counterparts, the Olympics "enjoyed mixing their sports with good conversation, wit, food and drink." The Philadelphia brand of baseball spread to other parts of Pennsylvania and even into Ohio and Kentucky. By the 1850s the Olympics were joined by two other Philadelphia clubs, the Athletics and the Excelsiors.

The game played by the Olympics was much closer to rounders than the New York game. There was no foul territory and no limit on the number of players. Instead of a diamond, the bases were laid out in a square much smaller than the modern baseball infield, with the batter standing between two bases in the baseline along one side of the square; the pitcher stood within the square and threw overhand. The ball was made of wood covered with leather and two kinds of bats were used: a flat, cricket-type bat for long hits and a small baseball-type bat that was swung with one hand and used to slap the ball away from opposing fielders backward or to the side.

Philadelphia town ball held out until May of 1860, when the Olympics became the last Philadelphia club to convert to the New York game. As a contemporary newspaper wrote,

Setting aside their time-honored play, endeared by the memories of thirty years, to press on in the race of progress, they adopted the National Association game of base ball, resulting in the honorable retirement of most of their old mem-

bers. Three hundred and sixty feet [the distance around the bases in baseball], compared with the old Town Ball circle of eighty feet, was enlarging their sphere of action with a vengeance.[1]

The Boston version of town ball, called the New England game, was very similar to the Philadelphia game, but it proved to be a much stronger rival to baseball Knickerbocker-style in the struggle to become the national game. The first Boston club was also called the Olympics and may also have grown out of games played by students. The game had had a long tradition at Boston English and Boston Latin high schools. The Boston Olympics were founded in 1854, and by 1857 they were playing matches on Boston Common against opponents named the Tri-Mountains, Green Mountains, Rough and Ready, Hancock, Bay State, Bunker Hill, and Wassapoag. Just as in New York and Brooklyn, the increasing popularity of the New England game led to disputes over rules, and in 1858 a general convention was held at Dedham, Massachusetts. The convention published a standard set of rules and established the Massachusetts Association of Base Ball Players.

One further reason for calling the Dedham convention was to defend against the growing influence of the New York game. Some New Englanders were already beginning to switch. The Tri-Mountains, which included E. G. Saltzman, a former second baseman for the New York Gothams, proposed to the convention that the New England clubs adopt the NABBP rules. Even though they were voted down, the Tri-Mountains and a club from Portland, Maine, staged an exhibition game on Boston Common to demonstrate the superiority of baseball New York-style. Portland won by a score of 47-42.

Like Philadelphia town ball, the New England game was played on a square with no foul territory. Pitchers threw overhand. Teams used lineups of ten to fifteen

47

players and the bases were wooden stakes four feet high. Fielders were called "scouts" and the pitcher was called the "thrower" or "giver." Base runners were put out by being "soaked" (hit by thrown balls) and fielders had to catch fly balls in the air, not on one bounce, in in order to put the batter out. Innings consisted of only one out. In spite of this, baseball New England-style featured even more runs than the New York game. According to the rules of 1858, a game was completed when one side scored one hundred "tallies," or runs.

For reasons that are not clear, the years 1857 and 1858 saw an explosion of interest in all sports all around the United States and Canada. Sparked by the Dedham convention, the New England game of baseball spread like wildfire, just as the New York game was spreading a couple of hundred miles to the south. Tremendous crowds turned out to see—and bet on— "Massachusetts state championship" matches played in 1859 by the Unions of Medway against the Winthrops of Holliston and in 1860 by the Unions against the Excelsiors of Upton. But in spite of their popularity, these matches demonstrated the chief reason why the New England game was soon to die out in favor of the New York version—it took too long. The 1859 game lasted two days and 101 innings; in the 1860 contest it took a cricketlike six days for one side to score the necessary 100 tallies. In the words of one observer, "The time occupied in playing the game under such rules was, we think, rather too much of a good thing."[2]

There were other reasons why the New England game lost out. The New York game was faster-moving and at the same time more complex; the New England game simply could not match its drama. The diamond-shaped infield and foul territory made the game much more appealing to spectators by allowing them to stand closer to the action at home plate. By combining the force-out and the possibility of multiple base runners, the New York game made both offensive and defensive teamwork possible. Without them, exciting plays like the stolen base, double or triple plays, tag up, or hit-and-run could never have developed; certainly the wooden stakes that marked the bases in the New England game would have discouraged sliding.

Finally, New York City's emergence as the dominant commercial power on the East Coast helped promote its version of baseball. It did so indirectly by adding to the prestige of the New York game (as it did for everything else from New York), and directly by sending out base-ball-playing entrepreneurs to make converts across the nation. Mr. Saltzman of the Tri-Mountains is one example, but there are many others. Following the example of Alexander Cartwright, New Yorkers in search of new business opportunities took their favorite pastime, base-ball, to the West. Many of them were members of New York baseball clubs; ex-Knickerbockers, ex-Eagles, ex-Putnams, and ex-Excelsiors founded the first baseball clubs in such cities as Cincinnati, San Francisco, and Sacramento.

By 1860, the respected Bowdoin club of Boston de-fected to the NABBP game. Others followed and by the middle 1860s the New England game had ceased to exist. Unlike the Philadelphia game, however, the New England game left behind an important legacy. Some of the features and at least part of the spirit of the Boston version of baseball live on in baseball today. First there is the baseball itself. Like the ball used in the Major Leagues today, the New England ball was made of rubber or sometimes cork wrapped tightly with yarn and covered with stitched leather. It was nearly as lively as a modern baseball, and much livelier than the Knickerbocker ball, which resembled a modern softball.

The rules of the New England game also required that a fly ball be caught in the air, as in today's baseball, rather than on one bounce as the New York rules allowed. This was known in the 1850s and 1860s as the "fly game." Henry Chadwick, the New York Knickerbockers, and others saw the superiority of the fly game and fought a long battle to have it adopted by the NABBP. In 1864 the association finally gave in and passed the fly ball rule that we still use today.

Another legacy of the New England game is overhand pitching. Even though, like New York pitchers, New England game pitchers were discouraged from trying too hard to get opposing batters out, it is obvious from contemporary descriptions that they often did just that. Sometimes they threw the ball very, very fast. In terms that are familiar to the modern fan, a contemporary newspaper story from the 1850s describes the thrill of watching one pitcher-batter confrontation on the Boston Common as follows: "[The pitcher] threw with a vigor . . . that made [the ball] whistle through the air, and stop with a solid smack in the catcher's hands."[3] Other observers describe crowds gathering at the Common to marvel at the spectacle of strong young men pitching hard and swinging from the heels. This was something entirely missing from the New York game, which required the pitcher to feed the ball to the hitter as gently as possible. Even though NABBP pitchers began to throw the ball faster and faster and from higher and higher arm angles in the 1860s and 1870s, it was not until the 1890s that baseball completely recaptured the thrill of overhand power pitching against power hitting that provides so much of the fun of the game today.

*B*ritish Invasion: Cricket and Father Chadwick

The New York game's defeat of town ball and the New England game in the 1850s was not the end of the story. There remained one final rival for baseball to overcome before it could be called America's national sport. That rival was not another variety of baseball. It was— believe it or not—cricket.

Today, no sport seems more English—or less American—than cricket. Cricket is played almost exclusively in Great Britain and former British colonies such as Australia, India, Pakistan, and Jamaica. Most Americans tend to dismiss it as a silly game played for days on end by men in white suits who break for tea. Few baseball fans have ever seen cricket played.

In the 1820s and 1830s, however, cricket was by far America's most popular sport. As far back as the middle 1700s, cricket clubs had been playing matches in Boston and New York. One reason for this was that America was full of immigrants from Great Britain who had arrived here already knowing how to play the game. Another was that there was no native American

51

sport to compete with it. None of the precursors of baseball—town ball, the New England game, or New York Knickerbocker–style baseball—had even got started until the late 1830s and 1840s.

Cricket arrived in America in the seventeenth century, with the first English settlers. Derived from a game played by shepherds in southeastern England during the Middle Ages, it had a history as an adult sport going back more than two centuries. Cricket was played enthusiastically by the respectable middle and upper classes throughout England in the late 1600s. By the year 1700, English noblemen were sponsoring or even playing in cricket matches. Eighteenth-century English newspapers routinely covered important matches and published statistics. Before Alexander Cartwright ever picked up a bat or a ball, cricket had developed a sophisticated set of rules and had already experienced the gambling scandals, conflicts over professionalism, and other problems that inevitably plague games once they have become money-making sports.

Alive and well on this side of the Atlantic in the 1830s, cricket benefited from the same North American sports boom that saw the rapid expansion of baseball's Philadelphia, New England, and New York versions. Cricket maintained its leading position on the American sports scene with the founding of the popular New York-based St. George Cricket Club, or "Dragonslayers," in 1838; the New York Cricket Club in 1840; and the Union Cricket Club of Philadelphia in 1843. By the middle 1850s, the two New York clubs had a lively rivalry going and both Boston and Philadelphia had thriving cricket scenes. Even Western cities like Cincinnati, Chicago, and Milwaukee boasted competitive cricket clubs. "By 1855," according to historian Marvin Adelman, "cricket was still more frequently played and attracted more public attention than baseball."

A baseball game being played on a former cricket field on Staten Island, N.Y.

The newspapers that would later do so much to promote baseball, including the *Spirit of the Times* and the *New York Clipper*, which in the 1850s used the subtitle the *Cricketers' Chronicle*, treated the various early versions of baseball the way modern newspapers treat yachting and polo. Cricket got the headlines; baseball scores and stories were buried deep in the fine print at the bottom of the page. To American fans of the time, the biggest sporting event of the 1840s was not the New York Knickerbockers' first match against the New York Nine at Hoboken. It was the United States–Canada cricket series of 1845 and 1846. While the

Knickerbockers were worrying about how to get eighteen club members to show up consistently on game days, the U.S.–Canada cricket match was drawing crowds of over five thousand spectators, who bet, according to contemporary reports, more than fifty thousand dollars on the outcome.

Like their baseball-playing counterparts in New York and Boston, the American cricket clubs held annual conventions in 1857, 1858, 1859, and 1860. While these conventions represented more players and more clubs, and were certainly more "national" than the New York or Boston baseball conventions, they probably did as much to weaken as to strengthen cricket's claim to being America's national game.

One problem was that the cricket conventions were torn apart by embarrassing internal conflicts and snobberies. New York and Philadelphia bickered over which city deserved the status of capital of American cricket. The two leading New York cricket clubs could not get along either. They waged a long and bitter feud which ended with the clubs refusing to take the field against each other. While baseball was opening up to the newer clubs and building the NABBP into a progressive and democratic body, the older cricket clubs like the two New York clubs were vying to dominate American cricket on the model of the Marylebone Cricket Club in London, which ruled—and still rules today—over the sport of cricket like a king.

The records of the cricket conventions of the 1850s show that American cricketers were very aware that their sport's biggest drawback was its Englishness. A lot of time was spent debating how to overcome this problem by somehow "Americanizing" the game. As Daniel Baker of Newark, New Jersey, said at the 1857 convention: "There are many things connected with the game which Americans could never understand. They knew only that it was an English game, and that was enough not to touch it."[1] Baker and others wanted to solve this problem by writing a new American set of rules for cricket, but they were voted down by traditionalists.

Some Americans, mostly from the Eastern states and from the upper classes, felt a close connection to England and English culture. Among many others, however, there was still considerable resentment left over from the American Revolution and the War of 1812, the two wars America had fought to gain independence from the English king.

America was also experiencing a rising tide of anti-foreign, anti-immigrant feeling. This was expressed politically by the founding of the Know Nothing party in 1853. The Know Nothings, whose name comes from their secretiveness—party members were supposed to say that they "knew nothing" if questioned about their activities—pushed for laws ending naturalization of immigrants and barring immigrants from political office. Americans of the 1840s and 1850s were in no mood to enjoy a sport in which native cricketers were regularly beaten by English-born players.

There were other problems with cricket as well. Americans were impatient with cricket's notorious complexities and eccentricities. The sport was also expensive. Because cricket bowlers (pitchers) bounce the ball once on the ground on its way to the batter—using spins and changes of pace to affect the way the ball acts after it hits the ground—the maintenance of a proper playing surface is all important.

To a much greater degree than in other outdoor sports, the wrong kind of grass, poor drainage, or any other kind of grounds problem can drastically affect or even ruin a cricket game. In England, playing fields had been set aside for cricket and lovingly cared for for centuries. It turned out to be very difficult to replicate these kinds of playing conditions in America, where people were used to enjoying a game of rounders, town ball, or baseball on any available street, farmer's field, or vacant lot. As one nineteenth-century English visitor to America put it, "Baseball requires no grass, as the ball does not touch the ground between the pitcher and the batter." Some early American cricket clubs had to disband when members could not afford their high grounds-keeping bills.

In the end, however, cricket failed in America, just as Daniel Baker had feared, because of its foreignness. Baseball in the 1850s may have been far behind cricket in sophistication, tradition, even in the number of par-ticipants—some historians estimate that there were as many as ten thousand active American cricketers in 1860—but baseball was coming up fast and its potential was unlimited. The same could not be said for cricket. No matter how many American cricket clubs there were or how well they played, there would always be a large percentage of the American people who would never accept a game imported from Europe. There was a sense in the late 1850s that it was time, as one news-paper put it, "to set up a game that could be termed a 'national American sport.'" For many Americans, that sport had to be 100 percent American.

In 1859 the All-England Eleven came to America for a series of three matches against American cricketers. The newspaper accounts of this tour give us a window on changing American attitudes toward baseball and cricket during this pivotal time. The All-England team was a national all-star team that included the very best cricketers in England and, therefore, the world. It was led by captain George Parr, the greatest batsman (hitter) of his time. Nicknamed the "Lion of the North," Parr came from the cricket hotbed of Nottinghamshire in northern England. The excitement caused in America by this visit from the world's greatest cricket team was comparable to the hoopla surrounding the appearance of the first American basketball "Dream Team" at the Barcelona Olympics.

On the surface, the 1859 All-England tour seemed to be a big success for cricket in America. American newspapers had stirred up great public interest by appealing to patriotism. "We whip the British in most things," editorialized the *Spirit of the Times,* "why should we not be able to 'try it on' at cricket?" The Stevens family spent two thousand dollars on refurbishing the cricket grounds at Elysian Fields, where one of the matches was to be played.

Huge crowds turned out to see the matches. Even though the English thoroughly outclassed their American opponents, returning undefeated from matches at Hoboken, Philadelphia, and Rochester, New York, the American sporting press remained positive. Instead of dwelling on the losses, sportswriters congratulated the Philadelphia squad that had lost to the English by the narrowest margin. American cricketers expressed optimism that, by giving American fans a taste of the sport at its finest, the series would "give great impetus to cricket in this hemisphere."

There was only one discordant note. That came when the newborn National Association of Base Ball Players had the nerve to challenge the All-England team to a best-two-out-of-three series of baseball games against a New York all-star team. This was no empty publicity stunt; the National Association put up the large sum of five thousand dollars to cover the All-England team's expenses. The English laughed off the American challenge, calling baseball the "schoolboy sport of rounders" and dismissing it as too simple for serious athletes to bother with. When pressed for a yes or no answer to the baseball challenge, the All-England team stalled by asking for even more money and then begged off. Before returning home, one member revealed that the cricketers had more respect for baseball than they let on. He was willing to play the Americans at their "schoolboy" game, he explained, if given "twelve months to practice at it."

This display of self-confidence by baseball served as a warning shot fired across the bow of the American cricket establishment. Few realized it at the time, but in spite of all the optimism of 1859, cricket in the United States was doomed. When the Civil War came a year later, the development of both cricket and baseball in America was put on hold for five years as the nation's young men went off to war. This wartime drought devastated both sports, but it also showed that the newer sport of baseball had sunk far deeper roots into American culture. When peace came, soldiers everywhere took off their uniforms and returned to the baseball diamond. The NABBP picked up right where it had left off, resuming its annual conventions and admitting dozens of new clubs each year. Most cricket clubs, on the other hand, did not resume play. Many of their members switched to baseball. The sport never regained the momentum of the 1850s. The Civil War finished cricket's chance of becoming a major sport in America.

Cricket may have lost out in its battle with baseball to become the national pastime, but, like the New England game, it did not disappear without a trace. Cricket made a lasting contribution to baseball by serving as a sort of role model or older brother to the younger sport. Without the influence of cricket, baseball would have been a very different game. A case could be made that without cricket, baseball might never have existed at all. Cricket directly influenced the development of baseball, starting with the original New York Knickerbockers. Alexander Cartwright and the other early baseball pioneers used American cricket clubs as organizational models. Cricket helped weaken American prejudices against sports in general by showing how athletics could be a serious, adult pursuit, and not just overgrown child's play. Cricket exemplified Victorian values, such as teamwork, self-discipline, courage, and rigorous practice, that were highly respected on both sides of the Atlantic. In their written constitutions and in their codes of rules, the Knickerbockers and other early baseball clubs stressed these same values.

The early New York City baseballers borrowed the idea of underhand pitching from the English. Cricket bowlers did not begin to throw overhand until the late 1890s—roughly the same time that overhand pitching came into vogue in baseball. Baseball borrowed much of its terminology from cricket. As late as the 1860s, cricket terms such as "batsman" for hitter, "side" for team, and "innings" for inning were still commonly used in base-ball. They also took the ideas of the umpire, the official scorer, and the importance of statistics themselves from cricket. The first box scores and the first baseball statistics were lifted directly from the cricket pages.

Finally, cricket paved the way for baseball by fostering a symbiotic, or mutually beneficial, relationship between sports and the newspapers. In the 1850s sports-oriented papers or newspapers with sports sections had hit upon the idea of trying to increase sales by vigorously pro-moting cricket. Even though cricket failed in the end, sports coverage, with its daily diet of numbers and game stories, did turn out to be an effective way for newspapers to attract and hold loyal readers. When baseball took cricket's place on the American sports scene, newspapers such as the *Spirit of the Times* and the *New York Clipper* found it easy to switch over to baseball. Baseball statistics and box scores replaced cricket statistics and box scores.

Cricket's greatest gift to baseball, however, was a man. His name was Henry Chadwick.

The son of a newspaper editor, Chadwick was born in Exeter, England, in 1824. He immigrated to the United States in 1837, when he was thirteen. Chadwick

Henry Chadwick, the first baseball journalist and inventer of the box score

loved to write; he also loved cricket. In 1843 he found a way to combine the two, taking a job as the cricket reporter for the *Long Island Star*. Later, he covered the cricket beat for other newspapers, including *The New York Times*. Throughout his twenties and early thirties Chadwick played an active role in the effort to popularize cricket in America.

Then in 1856 Chadwick dropped cricket and switched over to baseball after an experience that had overtones of a religious conversion. It happened while Chadwick was on a trip to Hoboken to cover a cricket match for the *Times*. As he tells the story himself in his 1868 book, *The Game of Baseball*:

> *It was in 1856, I think, when, on returning from the early close of a cricket match on Fox Hill, I chanced to go through the Elysian Fields during the progress of a contest between the noted Eagle and Gotham clubs. The game was being sharply played on both sides, and I watched it with deeper interest than any previous ball match between clubs that I had seen. It was not long before I was struck with the idea that base ball was just the game for a national sport for Americans, and, reflecting on the subject, it occurred to me, on my return home, that from this game of ball a powerful lever might be made by which our people could be lifted into a position of more devotion to physical exercise and healthful out-door recreation than they had hitherto, as a people, been noted for. At that period—and it is but eleven years ago—I need not state that out-door recreation was comparatively unknown to the large mass of the American people. In fact, as is well known, we were the regular target for the shafts of raillery and even abuse from our out-door sport-loving cousins of England, in consequence of our national neglect of sports and pastimes, and our too great devotion to business and the "Almighty Dollar." But thanks to Base Ball—the entering wedge of the great transformation which has since taken place—we have been transformed into quite another people. From the time that I first became*

an admirer of base ball, I have devoted myself to improving and fostering the game in every way I thought likely to promote the main object I had in view, viz: to assist in building up a national game for the country as much so as cricket is for England.[3]

Chadwick convinced his editor at the *Times* to allow him to cover a few baseball matches as an experiment. The experiment was a success and soon Chadwick was covering the booming sport of baseball for a staggering number of newspapers and magazines across the country.

Many contemporaries felt that Chadwick's coverage was part of the reason for baseball's boom. From the mid-1850s through the first decade of the twentieth century, he tirelessly promoted the sport. In 1858 Chadwick became history's first baseball editor, at the sports weekly the *New York Clipper*. In the 1860s he wrote for the *Brooklyn Eagle*, the *New York Herald* and the *New York Sun* and edited *Beadle's Dime Base Ball Player*, an influential annual, and *DeWitt's Baseball Guide*. From 1867 to 1869 he edited the first all-baseball weekly, *The Ball Player's Chronicle*, and in the 1880s edited the first fan publication, a New York City weekly entitled *The Metropolitan: A Journal of the Polo Grounders*. It was also in the 1880s that Chadwick began to edit the *Spalding Guide* series, which served as baseball's official annual for half a century.

Chadwick also authored several books. Among them were instructionals like the 1880 *The Art of Batting and Base Running* and the 1868 combination history and instructional *The Game of Baseball*, both of which taught generations of youngsters how to field, pitch, and hit. Chadwick's immense personal collection of scrapbooks, clippings, and statistics formed the basis for Albert Spalding's history, *Base Ball: America's National Game*, which was published a few years after Chadwick's death. Spalding's book paid tribute to Henry Chadwick's great contributions to the game and eulogized him as the "Father of Baseball."

While baseball certainly had many fathers, Henry Chadwick is far more deserving than Abner Doubleday, Alexander Cartwright, and most of the other men who have borne that title. More than a mere popularizer of baseball, Chadwick shaped and guided the young sport through the evolution of its rules and its early crises. Serving for more than a decade as the chairman of the NABBP rules committee, he led the fight to eliminate the rule that allowed fielders to catch fly balls on one bounce and fought for a series of rules changes that favored pitchers, lowered scoring to more modern levels, and generally made the game more difficult.

Chadwick saw himself as a protector of baseball and as a sort of reformer before the fact, through whom baseball would learn from the experiences of the older sport of cricket.

Most of Chadwick's efforts can be categorized as aimed at either raising baseball to the sophistication level of cricket or at helping baseball avoid some of the pitfalls encountered by cricket in its long history. In the first category would be Chadwick's promotion of pitching and fielding over hitting. For Chadwick, tight defense and tough pitching made for a more sophisticated, or in Chadwick's favorite phrase, a more "scientific and manly" game. In his annuals Chadwick would list the "notable" contests of the previous season; these were usually the same as the lowest-scoring games. He showed a cricketlike disapproval of swinging for the fences. "Long hits are showy," he wrote in 1868, "but they do not pay in the long run. Sharp grounders insuring the first-base certain . . . are worth all the hits made for home-runs which players strive for." Baseball showed the clear imprint of Chadwick's values until the home run revolution, led by Babe Ruth in the 1920s, came along and blasted the stolen base, the hit and run, the bunt, and the rest of "scientific" baseball into oblivion. Chadwick would despise baseball as it is played today: "Just think of the monotony," he wrote in 1891, "of a game marked by a series of home runs."

Chadwick the reformer served as baseball's conscience for over fifty years. Out of concern for the dignity and public image of the sport, Chadwick pushed for respect for umpires on the field as well as for better discipline for the players off the field. A man of great personal austerity—Chadwick began every morning with a 5 A.M. cold water plunge, after which he put in a twelve-hour workday—he sponsored the 1859 ban on postgame banquets and led a lifelong campaign against the mixture of alcohol and baseball. A typical Chadwick antidrinking sermon from an 1876 baseball annual reads:

> *Any man now desirous of using his physical and mental powers to the utmost advantage, must ignore first, intemperance in eating and second, refuse to allow a drop of alcoholic liquor, whether in the form of spirits, wine or beer, to pass down his throat.*[4]

For much of his life Chadwick fought Sunday baseball and creeping gambling-related corruption in the game. Even though he won the battle to have pool-selling (a popular form of gambling in the nineteenth century) banned at ballparks in 1876, Chadwick was not particularly successful in either area. Sunday baseball was legal in most Major League cities by the late 1910s and the ban on pool-selling was followed a year later by the Louisville affair, a game-fixing scandal second in baseball history only to the Black Sox scandal of 1919. Chadwick tolerated the growth of professionalism in baseball during the 1850s and 1860s but railed against players who "revolved," or jumped from one team to another in search of a better contract, a problem which had caused a great deal of trouble in English cricket.

Henry Chadwick's most lasting contribution to baseball may be his influence on scoring and statistics. Chadwick was obsessed with developing and maintaining accurate and useful baseball statistics to measure the ways in which individual players contribute to team performance. Because so much of the fun of baseball lies in comparing the records and numbers of players from different eras, without Chadwick's efforts much of the game's interest and most of its history would be lost.

Some of baseball's early statistics were adapted by Chadwick from cricket; others were pure Chadwick innovations. It was Chadwick who, in the 1850s and early 1860s, borrowed the scorecard and the box score from cricket. He also appropriated cricket's main offensive statistic, the runs-per-game average, as a way to measure individual batting effectiveness. It was not long, however, before Chadwick's restless intelligence focused on improving all three and making them better suited for baseball. By 1876, after a series of modifications, he had perfected the baseball box score. Chadwick's 1876 model could still be found, unchanged, in newspaper sports sections of the 1950s.

Chadwick also soon realized that cricket's runs-per-game average was not a good way to measure hitting in baseball. This was because in cricket a run is the same thing as a base hit—because there is only one base not occupied by the batsman (batter), to reach base is to score a run. In baseball, runs tend to be built by stringing together a series of hits; in most cases the man who physically crosses the plate does not necessarily deserve all—or even most—of the credit for producing the run. The runs-per-game statistic gave batters no credit for reaching base when the following batters failed to drive them in, or for hits that moved runners into scoring position, or for hits that drove runs in. Chadwick's answer was to invent a new average called hits per game, which was later refined as hits per at-bat. This, of course, is our modern batting average.

Over the decades, Chadwick experimented with other statistics, publishing the more successful ones in his baseball annuals. Henry Chadwick invented or perfected the vast majority of official stats in use today, including slugging average and on-base average, earned run average, defensive putouts and assists, errors, earned and unearned runs, and total bases.

Chadwick died at the age of eighty-four in 1908; he had still been working as a sportswriter. He was buried beneath a granite monument in Brooklyn's picturesque Greenwood Cemetery. In 1938 Chadwick became a member of the select first group to be inducted into the National Baseball Hall of Fame in Cooperstown, New York. He remains the only baseball writer to be honored not in the writers' wing but in the main hall, alongside Babe Ruth, Walter Johnson, Joe DiMaggio, Jackie Robinson, and the rest of the all-time greats of the game.

CHAPTER SIX

Ferryboat Series: The Game Becomes a Sport

For more than a century, baseball writers and historians have argued about when and where baseball really began. According to Albert Spalding, the game was invented by Abner Doubleday in Cooperstown in 1839. A lot depends, of course, on what you mean by baseball. Some scholars have argued that baseball-type games date back over a thousand years earlier than that, to the beginnings of Anglo-Saxon culture, or even as far back as the time of the pharaohs of ancient Egypt. Most historians today agree that Alexander Cartwright and the Knickerbockers invented a game that is the direct ancestor of modern baseball around the year 1846.

Henry Chadwick had a different opinion. It was always his position that baseball began in 1857. Chadwick was referring specifically to the winter baseball convention held in New York City after the close of the 1857 season, which he attended. "The changes in the rules introduced...in 1857," he maintained, "were such as to materially improve the game." These rules changes distinguished it from baseball Knickerbocker-style, which

Chadwick found "tediously dull and uninteresting" by comparison.

The 1857 rules, which took effect at the start of the 1858 season, address many of the ambiguities and omissions of the fairly crude original twenty-one Knickerbocker rules. They are much more detailed and precise, taking up at least four or five times as much printed space. Among other things, they appoint a single neutral umpire instead of the three-man committee of the Knickerbocker era; specify the duties of the umpire and the official scorer; introduce canvas bases; and endorse the 1856 rule change that limited games to nine innings.

The 1857 convention was also important because it created the National Association of Base Ball Players. The NABBP and its rules committee made possible not only the improved 1857 rules, but all of the refinements of the following decade, including the adoption of the fly game, the gradual introduction of called balls and strikes, and the rule allowing runners to tag up after a catch.

The year 1857 was also a turning point in more profound ways. Beginning in New York, Brooklyn, and a few other northeastern cities during the late 1850s, baseball was undergoing a great transformation from a participant sport to a spectator sport. As late as 1856, Henry Chadwick saw baseball chiefly as a way to promote "physical exercise and healthful out-door recreation." Only a few years later, however, baseball took off as a form of popular entertainment. Many Americans of the late 1850s and early 1860s belonged to baseball clubs; many more followed the game in the sports pages, rooted for their favorite players, and bet on their local teams. Baseball was becoming less and less something Americans *did*—like, say, modern softball—and more and more something they *watched*—like Major League baseball.

Once restricted to a closed circle of club players and their friends, the baseball world now had to make room for unheard-of numbers of nonplaying fans. Not personally acquainted with the players on the field, fans tend to idolize players. As we do with today's sports, music, or film stars, fans of the late 1850s and 1860s turned their favorite baseball players into larger-than-life celebrities.

Fans changed the game in almost every way. Fan identification with players increased the competitive stakes. Booming fan interest in baseball stars and fan-driven regional rivalries put pressure on players to win not just for themselves, but for their fans, neighborhoods, boroughs, or cities. This pressure to win seriously weakened baseball's amateur ethic. Even though NABBP rules continued strictly to forbid professionalism of any kind, starting around 1860 teams began to pay their star players anyway.

The advent of baseball fans also raised the stakes literally, by bringing more and more money into the game. Fans bought newspapers and baseball publications in order to follow their favorite players or teams. A new cast of characters appeared who saw sports not as a pastime but as an industry. Owners of baseball grounds sold admission tickets and professional book-makers and pool-sellers openly took bets right in the stands during games. Men like ballplayer-turned-entrepreneur Mort Rogers—who at Boston parks in 1871 sold the first scorecards—and many others who had never pitched a ball or swung a bat, set up concessions selling food, drink, and transportation to greater and greater crowds.

The first baseball cards date from this period. Called by the French term *cartes de visite*, or visiting cards, these cards were one of the early commercial forms of photography, which had been invented in 1839. About one and a half times the size of today's cards, they depicted individual players or entire teams, usually posing stiffly with an assortment of baseball equipment in a set consisting of a floor with an Oriental carpet pattern and either a plain backdrop or an outdoor scene painted on canvas. Intended for use as souvenirs or promotions, *cartes de visite* were handed out by individuals, photography studios, or other businesses. Sporting goods manufacturers and tobacconists were among the first businesses to sponsor the cards. *Cartes de visite* were the forerunners both of modern baseball cards, which were given out first with packs of cigarettes or chewing tobacco and later with bubble gum, and of picture postcards. Like modern baseball cards, *cartes de visite* were collected, traded, and preserved in albums; they were also used to collect players' autographs.

The early 1860s would see the construction of the first baseball parks enclosed by fences. The reason for the fences was purely commercial: to limit the crowd to paying customers. This would lead years later to a huge unintended consequence that changed the game of baseball completely and forever—the home run.

These changes were gradual. But if you had to pick one time and place where baseball crossed the line from the friendly, completely amateur pastime of the Knickerbocker era into the intense, increasingly commercialized sport of the late 1850s and 1860s, the choice would be easy. The place would be Flushing, New York; the time: 2:30 in the afternoon of Tuesday, July 20, 1858.

Flushing is now a bustling, mostly Asian neighborhood in the middle of the borough of Queens in New York City. In 1858, however, it was a sleepy village on the north shore of what was then rural Long Island; most New Yorkers knew it only as the home of a horse-racing track called the Fashion Race Course. Named the National Race Course when it was built in 1854, the Fashion Course featured an immense stone grandstand

A baseball game in a fenced-in ballpark

that seated twelve thousand spectators. In 1856 it was renamed after Fashion, the horse who, in 1842, had won the greatest of the "intersectional races," which matched the horse-racing champions of the North and South. Neither the grandstand nor the new name helped; racing fans found the track too difficult to reach from Manhattan, and by 1857 it had fallen into disuse and disrepair. Coincidentally, the Fashion Course was located in a part of Flushing known as Willets Point, only a few hundred yards from the present site of Shea Stadium, the home of today's New York Mets.

On that Tuesday afternoon in 1858, Flushing was anything but sleepy. Masses of excited baseball fans were streaming in from New York and Brooklyn by ferry, railroad car, and horse-drawn carriage. By 2:00 P.M. the

Fashion Course grandstand hosted a crowd estimated at between fifteen hundred and four thousand, by far the largest number of people who had ever gathered to watch a baseball game anywhere. "No race day the Fashion Course has ever seen," gushed *Porter's Spirit of the Times,* "presented such a brilliant numerical array...the *coup d'oeil* [visual effect] was brilliant in the extreme."[1]

The turnout was even more impressive considering that each fan was charged a fifty-cent admission fee. This was no small amount—in 1858 a men's haircut cost about ten cents. The charge was justified, according to the sponsoring committee of Joseph B. Jones of the Excelsiors, Thomas S. Dakin of the Putnams, and James W. Davis of the Knickerbockers, to pay for all of the work that had gone into sprucing up the grandstand and preparing the grounds for baseball.

This was the first known instance of baseball fans paying to watch a game, but admission charges would shortly become routine. Entrepreneurs in New York and Brooklyn were impressed by the large sums of money raised by the Fashion Course games. In 1862 one of them, William Cammeyer, built the Union Grounds, the first permanent enclosed ballpark, at the corner of Lee Avenue and Rutledge Street in Williamsburg, Brooklyn. Cammeyer made his park available to Brooklyn baseball clubs for free but made a nice profit by charging fans ten cents to see the games. Within five years, most teams were playing in fenced-in parks where admission was charged.

What brought so many eager fans out to Flushing on that Tuesday in 1858? The answer could be found splashed across the top of the sports section of that day's *New York Tribune:*

GREAT BASEBALL MATCH—POSTPONEMENT
In consequence of the storm on Tuesday, 13th,
the Committee announces that the match will

take place on Tuesday, 20th inst., at the Fashion Course, near Flushing. Steamer Iolas leaves Fulton Market slip at 10 A.M. and 1 P.M. to connect with cars for the course. Extra stages will be furnished at the Peck Slip ferry, Williamsburgh. Extra boats will be run on the Greenpoint Ferry, foot of 10th and 23rd Streets, New York.

The "Great Baseball Match" was the opening game of a best-two-out-of-three game series between all-star teams representing New York City, the baseball capital of the nation, and its chief rival, the city of Brooklyn. New York, of course, was the birthplace of the Knicker-bockers and the home of the baseball powers of the middle 1850s: the Eagle, Gotham, and Empire clubs. Along with the Unions of Morrisania, who were consid-ered a New York club even though they played in what is now the Bronx, these four clubs had long dominated the baseball scene.

Brooklyn, however, was coming up fast. The first competitive Brooklyn club was the Atlantics. Barely able to hold their own against the top New York clubs in 1856, the Atlantics went undefeated against them in 1857. Three other young clubs from Brooklyn, the Excelsiors, Eckfords, and Putnams, were also soon to be heard from. In 1858, for the first time, the top Brooklyn clubs won more games than they lost against New York opponents. Four of the top five clubs (as measured by won-lost record) were from the Brooklyn side of the East River; the Empires were the only New York club to hold its own against the four best Brooklyn clubs.

In those days, there was no official schedule, play-offs, or any other formal way to determine which New York-area team was the champion in a given season. In most years, champions were determined partly by con-sensus and partly by a sort of championship series. At first, the two teams generally considered to be the best would meet in a late-season best-two-games-out-of-

73

The Unions baseball team of Morrisania,
Bronx, N.Y., 1867 champions

three series, with the winner being declared "national champions." Later on, the championship would go to whoever defeated the previous year's champion in a best-two-out-of-three series. Even though Boston and other baseball-playing cities held their own regional championship series, the New York metropolitan area was still the center of the baseball universe. Since virtually all of the top clubs in the country played in New York or Brooklyn, the New York-area championship was equivalent to a national championship.

Intending to demonstrate to the world that they no longer took second place to New York City in baseball, in the spring of 1858 the upstart baseball powers from Brooklyn challenged the New Yorkers to a battle of all-stars to be played at the Fashion Course in the late summer. The New York clubs eagerly accepted.

Game one of the New York-Brooklyn all-star series had all of the excitement and hoopla of a New York

Yankee-Brooklyn Dodger World Series from the 1950s or the one-game showdown for the 1951 National League pennant between the Brooklyn Dodgers and the New York Giants—the game that was won by New York in the bottom of the ninth inning by Bobby Thomson's home run, nicknamed the "shot heard around the world."

A better analogy might be Bull Run, the first major battle of the Civil War, with the Brooklyn team playing the part of the Union troops. The Unions were so sure of an easy victory at Bull Run that they treated the battle as though it were a Fourth of July parade or a Boy Scout Outing. They brought "fans" along as well: well-dressed ladies and gentlemen from Washington, D.C., drove out in carriages and picnicked on the hillsides overlooking the battleground. The underdog Confederates ruined the party, however, by winning the battle in a rout and sending the panicked spectators scurrying back to Washington before they could finish their hors d'oeuvres and champagne.

When the baseball fans got off the train at Flushing station, they encountered a Coney Island atmosphere of "card sweaters" (three-card-monte artists) and "thimble-riggers" (shell-game operators). There were also "try your strength" machines, "guess your weight" games, and other carnival attractions. Inside the grandstand itself a more respectable tone prevailed. Besides the expected bookmakers, ballplayers, and young men, the Fashion Course crowd featured an unusual number of women. One reporter described a "galaxy of youth and beauty in female form who, smiling on the scene, nerved the players to their task, and urged them, like true knights of old, to do their devoirs before their 'ladyes fair.'"[2] Possibly for this reason, the 1858 fans seem to have been better behaved than their modern counterparts. A lone heckler was shamed into silence by a nearby fan who asked him with great sarcasm, "Are you a ball player, too?"

Heckling may not have been respectable in 1858, but gambling was. Bets were openly taken inside and outside the ballpark; even women were seen putting money down on their favorite side. As the predominantly pro-Brooklyn spectators settled in their seats and nervously awaited the first pitch, the odds were running 20-15 in favor of Brooklyn. Expecting a pitching and defensive duel, many fans bet that neither side would score as many as 12 runs.

The Brooklyn team was made up of two representatives each from the Excelsiors, Eckfords, and Putnams, and three players from the powerful Atlantic lineup. The biggest stars on the team were Excelsiors catcher J. B. Leggett, who, in those days before catcher's masks, was known for his courage in grabbing "balls sharp from the bat"; Eckford captain Frank Pidgeon; and the O'Brien brothers: Pete, known as "The Old War Horse," and Matty. The Brooklynites may well have been overconfident. Instead of using a batting order based on the skills of the hitters, they took turns batting by club affiliation; the two Excelsiors batted first, followed by the two Eckfords, followed by the Atlantics, and so on.

The New York squad featured players from the Unions, Empires, Eagles, Gothams, and Knickerbockers. They had less talent but used a more rational batting order. The most notable name in the New York lineup is that of young Harry Wright of the Knickerbockers, who played right field. Then a twenty-three-year-old cricketer playing his first season of baseball, Wright would soon develop into one of the finest players of the day. He was also an innovative tactician. Toward the end of his playing days, Wright would single-handedly invent the art of managing a baseball team.

For the first three and a half innings, the game was all Brooklyn. Brooklyn's defense then fell apart without warning in the middle innings and squandered a 7-3 lead, as New York scored a total of thirteen runs in the

*J. B. Leggett, Excelsiors catcher and goat of the
1858 Fashion Course series*

fourth, fifth, and sixth. Most of these came on passed balls by catcher Leggett, who was having a tough day even by the standards of a time when catchers played without gloves or padding of any kind. Leggett was moved to the outfield after letting two in a row get by him with men on base in the eighth inning, but it was too late; New York base runners made a total of twelve bases on passed balls—eleven of them off poor Leggett, while Brooklyn made only two.

The favorites from Brooklyn raised their fans' hopes in the top of the eighth by scoring four times to recapture the lead, 18-17, but they gave the lead away for a second time in the bottom of the inning. New York scored five runs in the eighth inning and put the game away in the ninth with three spectacular catches. The final score was 22-18, New York.

The mostly pro-Brooklyn crowd was in a serious mood at the second game of the series, which was held at the Fashion Course on August 17. This time there was little gambling and nothing of the party atmosphere of game one. The players meant business, too. Gone was the slumping J. B. Leggett, as well as nearly every other Putnam or Excelsior; eight out of nine members of this Brooklyn team were from the stronger Eckford and Atlantic clubs. There were three Eckfords, including Frank Pidgeon, now pitching, and five Atlantics: Price, Oliver, the O'Brien brothers, and shortstop Dickey Pearce. Considered, along with Harry Wright's younger brother George, one of the first great shortstops, Dickey Pearce helped change the shortstop from a universal cutoff man on throws from the outfield into the most important member of the infield defense. He may also have invented the bunt. A skilled base runner, Pearce batted leadoff for the Atlantics during the late 1850s and 1860s, a time when they were far and away the best team in baseball.

The tactic of stacking the Brooklyn team with Atlantics succeeded brilliantly. Brooklyn scored six runs

*Dickey Pearce, shortstop of the Brooklyn Atlantics
and the Brooklyn All-Star Nine of 1858*

off New York pitcher Van Cott in the first inning and then slowly pulled away. All betting ceased by the fourth inning and Brooklyn coasted to a 29-8 victory.

The teams met for the deciding game of the match almost a month later on September 10th. In the 1911 history of baseball that he based partly on Henry Chadwick's scrapbooks, Albert Spalding gives the following account of game three of the Fashion Course series:

By this time a widespread interest in the result had sprung up in both cities, and something of the spirit of local partisanship which characterizes league games at the present time was apparent. The crowd in attendance upon this event was the largest that had ever been seen on a ball field, numbering several thousand...the fight for supremacy in this game was very bitter. Both teams were on their mettle, every player feeling that the future welfare of the city represented by him depended upon the result.[3]

This time Brooklyn brought out a team made up of three Eckfords and six members of the mighty Atlantics. This team was far superior to the New York team—on paper. But that day Brooklyn fans learned, like so many generations of fans to come, how little it can mean to be the winner of a baseball game "on paper." They went home disappointed for a second time. Their team gave up seven runs in the first inning and never got back into the contest, losing by a final score of 29-18. New York had won the series, two games to one, and temporarily reasserted its baseball supremacy.

Very temporarily, as it turned out—the following season Brooklyn had all four of the top clubs in won-lost record, with the Atlantics once again leading the way. It would be nearly a decade before a club not named Atlantic, Excelsior, or Eckford would win the consensus national championship. In 1863, the Eckfords accomplished the unique feat of winning every single game they played; their second nine and "amateur nine" went undefeated as well. In baseball, Brooklyn was now king.

The brand of baseball played in the Fashion Course series of 1858 was a far cry from modern baseball. It retained many of the more ragged aspects of the game of the Knickerbocker era. Few players specialized in only one position; most were generalists, moving frequently from one position to another. Fielders made a lot of errors and dropped a lot of fly balls. Of the outs in game one, for instance, 50 percent were made on balls caught on one bounce—if the two teams had been playing by Henry Chadwick's "fly game" rule, the games might never have ended! The two teams also held Knickerbockeresque parties and toasting sessions after each game. And certainly, no modern baseball club would do something as silly as to organize a batting order by what club the players came from.

Still, the Fashion series marked a great leap forward toward modern baseball for three reasons: because it showed that baseball could make money, because it helped create baseball's first generation of real stars, and because it was a great event that captured the imagination of the public beyond the small baseball world of the time. Thanks to the publicity and excitement generated by the 1858 Fashion Course series, baseball was becoming something more than a game. It was becoming part-game and part-business—in other words, a sport like our modern sports.

Baseball's next great event, the Brooklyn Excelsiors national tour, took place two years later. Like the Fashion Course series, the Excelsiors tour electrified baseball fans across the country and created new stars. One of these new stars was even bigger than Dickey Pearce, Harry Wright, or the O'Briens. His name was Jim Creighton. He was baseball's first national hero.

Creighton was born in New York City in 1841 but was raised across the river in Brooklyn. An accomplished infielder at the age of sixteen, he had helped organize a junior club called Young America in 1857; the following year he and a friend formed the Niagaras, another junior club. Creighton was also a terrific hitter.

It was during the early part of the 1859 season that Jim Creighton, who had some experience as a cricket bowler, began to experiment with pitching. While trying out different deliveries, he hit upon a way of getting more power from his hips and snapping his wrist in a subtle way that did not seem to violate the pitching rules. The rules of that time required a pitcher to toss the ball dead underhand, using a smooth motion and without making any turn or jerk of the wrist. Using his new delivery in a game against the Stars, a famous junior club that was used as a sort of farm team by the Excelsiors, Creighton caused a sensation. "On the final inning of the game when the Stars were a number of runs ahead," runs one account of the event,

> The Niagaras changed pitchers, and Jimmy took that position. Peter O'Brien [the famous Atlantics star] witnessed this game, and when Creighton got to work something new was seen in baseball—the low swift delivery, the ball rising from the ground past the shoulder to the catcher. The Stars soon saw that they could not cope with such pitching.[4]

When the Stars managed to make contact at all with Creighton's pitches, they popped them up for easy outs. Anyone who has faced a good modern fast-pitch softball pitcher knows how the Stars hitters felt.

Creighton was recruited by the Stars and by opening day of the 1860 season he was pitching for the Excelsiors. Creighton was controversial in many ways. Many claimed that his pitching motion was illegal, but they were overruled by Henry Chadwick, who welcomed Creighton's new style of pitching. It fit perfectly into Chadwick's program of making hitting more difficult and the game in general more "scientific and manly." Others whispered that the Excelsiors were paying Creighton to pitch for them in violation of the NABBP's amateur ethic. This was most likely true, although the association did nothing about it.

By the end of the 1860 season, Jim Creighton had become baseball's biggest attraction. He was especially loved by the young. It seemed that every boy in the early 1860s dreamed of playing like their hero, the way today's young fans dream of becoming Barry Bonds or Ken Griffey, Jr. Junior clubs were filled with boys who imitated Creighton's every mannerism; a number of these clubs even named themselves after him. It is possible that the baseball expression "phenom," meaning a terrific young prospect, was coined to describe Creighton. Fittingly, the earliest known prototype of the baseball *carte de visite*—in a sense, the first baseball card—is a Jim Creighton card from 1863.

The Jim Creighton legend began on June 30, 1860, when he and the Excelsiors left Brooklyn on a train bound for Albany, a city located more than a hundred miles up the Hudson River. The Excelsiors had scheduled two weeks' worth of matches against teams from Albany and nearby Troy, and from towns across upstate New York. Today, of course, there is nothing unusual about baseball teams going on the road. Exhibition games far away from home, spring training trips to the South or Latin America, as well as in-season road trips, are all common features of professional baseball. In 1860, however, baseball clubs rarely traveled farther than they could go by horse-drawn carriage or ferryboat in one day. The Excelsiors were the first baseball team anywhere to make a true cross-country baseball tour.

The Excelsiors' tour was made possible by two new developments. One was the rapid expansion of America's railroad system, which made the tour physically possible. In 1840 there had been a total of 2,818 miles of railroad track in the entire country; most of it was concentrated in the Northeast. By 1850 this had increased only to 7,500 miles; it was not until 1853 that New York and Chicago were linked by rail. During the late 1850s, however, the nation's railroads underwent a dizzying expansion. By 1860 total track mileage had jumped to

29,000 miles, most of it still on the northeastern seaboard and in the upper Midwest. By making it much easier and faster to move troops and supplies long distances, the superiority of the railroad system in the North proved to be a key ingredient in the Union's victory over the South in the Civil War. On May 10, 1869, the first transcontinental railroad line was completed; it was now possible to travel between the East and West coasts by train.

The other new development was a tremendous increase in the popularity of baseball outside New York, Boston, and Philadelphia. Across upstate New York, into the Midwest and down South, hundreds of new baseball clubs were formed by enthusiastic new players who looked East—to the famous New York and Brooklyn clubs—for their models. In 1860 the Brooklyn Excelsiors, thanks in large part to the pitching of Jim Creighton, were on their way to dethroning the Atlantics as New York-area champions. When the Excelsiors announced their mid-summer tour, dozens of young "country clubs" lined up for the honor of playing against the finest team in baseball.

The Excelsiors' tour may have been the first modern-style road trip, but in many ways it was a grander version of the old-fashioned home-and-away series of the Knickerbocker era. Like the Knickerbockers, the Excelsiors were strict amateurs; they paid their own way and refused to take a penny from their host clubs. And while the Excelsiors played a hard-nosed, serious brand of baseball, they did accept their opponents' hospitality at elaborate postgame banquets and parties that rivaled those of the 1840s and early 1850s.

A crowd of over one thousand fans turned out for the Excelsiors' game against the Albany champions on July 2, 1860. It was no contest. Creighton and his teammates, who were described by one Troy newspaper as having "pretty well reduced base ball to a science," destroyed the Albany club by a score of 24-6. In the style of the time, the Albany players were good sports. "At the conclusion of the game," reported the *Albany Evening Journal*, "there was cheering on both sides and the ball was delivered to the winners. About 5 o'clock the Champions invited their guests to a glorious dinner at the Merchants Hotel where a happy time was had and the greatest good feeling was manifest."

After crossing the Hudson river to defeat a solid Troy club, 13-7, the Excelsiors traveled by train to Buffalo to play western New York's top club, the Niagaras. Buffalo fans were optimistic that their team could hold its own against the Excelsiors and eagerly put out the welcome mat. On the day before the game, Niagara players treated Creighton and his teammates to a July Fourth excursion to Niagara Falls and an elaborate banquet at the Clifton House on the Canadian side of the border. The Niagaras baseball grounds were completely renovated, with new wooden grandstands added to accommodate the four or five thousand fans expected to turn out.

By the time the Buffalo pitcher threw the first pitch of the game, fans had filled not only the new stands, but every roof, tree, and high window in the vicinity. But the Niagaras, who were touted by a local newspaper as "heretofore regarded as invincible," lost the game so badly that the city of Buffalo was left in a state of shock. Creighton was overpowering, J. B. Leggett scored a team-high eight runs, and the Excelsiors won 50-19, "the highest score," according to Albert Spalding, "that had ever been recorded in a [top-level] base ball match up to that date."

The Excelsiors went on to complete their northern tour with a record of 6-0; only Troy, a baseball hotbed that would be heard from later, managed to play a competitive game against them. The disappointment of the defeated clubs, however, soon gave way to a renewed determination to improve and become competitive with the Excelsiors and the other big-city clubs. As Albert Spalding writes:

> The triumphal tour of the Excelsiors had wrought wonders in the way of creating public sentiment favorable to the game. The contests...had inspired the young men of those cities to emulate the example of the youth of New York and Brooklyn, and had begotten within them the hope that they might win for their cities a glory akin to that which had been achieved for the city on Long Island. As a result, clubs were organized by the hundreds, the fever spreading to all parts of the country, East, West, North and South, and matches, which developed strong new players, were scheduled everywhere.[5]

After returning to Brooklyn, where they stunned the defending champion Atlantics, 23-4, in the first game of the 1860 championship series, the Excelsiors resumed their tour, this time heading south. The results were not much different from those of the northern phase of the trip. They crushed a Baltimore all-star team 51-6, enjoyed a "magnificent dinner at Guy's...at which flowers in profusion decorated the tables [and] toasts and songs abounded," and moved on by train to Philadelphia. There they beat another all-star team—made up of members of the Athletics, Olympics, and other local clubs, who had only recently switched from town ball to the New York game—by a score of 15-4.

The Excelsiors may have finished their tour undefeated, but they left their opponents more inspired than discouraged. "Like the New York tour," writes Spalding, "this trip had a tremendous influence in promoting the game in a new quarter." Baseball clubs everywhere wanted to try to solve Creighton's pitching and tame the mighty Excelsiors. When they returned to Brooklyn on the ninth of August for the second game of the Atlantics series, the Excelsiors learned that they had been invited to extend their tour with a series of games in Boston.

As it turned out, there was little glory left for Creighton's team in 1860. They put off the Boston trip until the following season. By then, however, the Civil War had broken out and the baseball world had entered a five-year period of dormancy. After losing many of their players to the Union army, most New York and Brooklyn clubs drastically cut back on their playing schedules during the war years. In 1861 the Excelsiors did not play at all.

The 1860 championship series ended inconclusively, because of an incident that illustrated the dark side of the explosion of new fan interest in baseball. In game two of the series, the Excelsiors, behind Creighton, were leading 12-3 after five innings and seemingly on their way to dethroning the champion Atlantics easily. But Creighton was ill. He weakened in the seventh, allowing nine runs, to give the O'Brien brothers and their Atlantics a 15-12 lead. After replacing Creighton on the mound, the Excelsiors came back in the eighth and ninth, but fell just short, losing 15-14.

The rubber match was held on August 23 at a neutral site, the Putnams' grounds in what is now the neighborhood of Bedford-Stuyvesant in Brooklyn. In the two weeks between games two and three, tensions among the baseball fans of Brooklyn and New York had reached the breaking point. An unprecedented amount of money was bet on the two teams. Some Atlantics supporters, who included large numbers of working-class and Irish immigrant fans, warned publicly that, if the game were close, they would "not permit" their team to lose. With typical delicacy, Spalding describes the atmosphere of the days leading up to the game:

The intense feeling of partisanship that had been engendered by the preceding contests increased...until it had become very bitter. It permeated all grades of society. Schoolboys, clerks, merchants, manufacturers, workingmen, and members of all the learned professions were profoundly interested. This would have been well enough, but, unfortunately, in those days all Eastern cities were noted for their utterly uncontrollable elements of thugs, gamblers, thieves, plug-uglies [gangsters] and rioters. Of these both New York and Brooklyn had more than their full quotas. It happened that public sympathy, as expressed in the views of the disorderly members of society, was strongly in favor of the Atlantics.[6]

With the Excelsiors leading in the fifth inning of the game, 8-6, behind a recovered Jim Creighton, the mood of the crowd, estimated by some observers to be fifteen thousand to twenty thousand strong, grew uglier and uglier. Atlantics fans tried to intimidate the Excelsiors with verbal abuse; they booed every close call that went against them and demanded that the umpire be replaced. Finally, they stormed the field and a general brawl broke out. The Brooklyn police had to be called in to restore order. At this point Leggett, the Excelsiors captain, took his team off the field and offered the ball—signifying victory—to Atlantics captain Pete O'Brien. No doubt, he expected O'Brien to refuse, considering that the Excelsiors were ahead in the game, and that it was the Atlantics' fans who had disrupted the game.

"Here, O'Brien, is the ball," Leggett said icily. "You can keep it."

"Will you call it a draw?" O'Brien replied.

"As you please" was Leggett's answer.

The Excelsiors were furious that the Atlantics did not concede the game. Neither the hard feelings between the two clubs nor the championship of 1860 was ever ultimately resolved. The Excelsiors and Atlantics never played baseball on the same field again.

Jim Creighton's career came to an even unhappier end. The Excelsiors played a limited schedule in 1862 and Creighton picked up where he had left off two years earlier. In an October 7 game against the Unions of Morrisania, however, Creighton suffered a freak accident. While Creighton was hitting a home run, the next batter heard a popping noise; Creighton later said that he had thought it was the sound of his belt snapping. By the time he had circled the bases, however, both Creighton and his teammates knew that something was wrong. Creighton had suffered a ruptured spleen or some other internal injury; he died eleven days later at his parents' home on Henry Street in Brooklyn Heights. According to his obituary, Creighton was "twenty-one years, seven months and two days" old.

Jim Creighton's career was so brief that his impact on his contemporaries is better measured by the tremendous outpouring of grief at his death than by the few statistics and game stories that make up what we know of his career. The Excelsiors erected a large granite monument, topped by a stone baseball, over his grave on Tulip Hill in Brooklyn's Greenwood Cemetery—not far from where Henry Chadwick would be laid to rest. The face of the monument, which stands today, contains a carving in relief of a pair of crossed bats, a cap, a base, and a scorebook labeled "Excelsior." The memory of baseball's first hero did not fade quickly. "Creighton ranked as the pitcher *par excellence* in baseball," wrote Henry Chadwick in 1868, "and there has been no one to equal him since he died." Considering how quickly the level of competition was improving during the 1860s, this is an amazing statement.

A portrait of the baseball world in
Frank Leslie's Illustrated Newspaper *of 1865.*
Bust in center is Jim Creighton.

For years after his death, Creighton's gravesite was the object of pilgrimages by baseball clubs visiting New York and Brooklyn. The Washington Nationals, for instance, stopped at Greenwood cemetery to pay their respects to Creighton between games against the Unions and Excelsiors in July 1866. The almost cultlike devotion of the baseball world to Jim Creighton's memory is shown in an engraving covering two pages from the November 4, 1865, edition of *Frank Leslie's Illustrated Newspaper.* The illustration depicts the New York-area baseball scene of the time. Flanking a panorama of a match in progress between the Atlantics and Eckfords at the Union Grounds in Brooklyn, beneath banners containing the names of the principal clubs of New York, Brooklyn, and New Jersey, are busts of T. C. Voorhis, president of the NABBP, and Henry Chadwick. Arranged along the top and bottom of the panorama are smaller, baseball card–like full-length portraits of top players, including J. B. Leggett, James W. Davis, Pete O'Brien, Mort Rogers and Thomas Dakin. Centered at the top of the page, however, and shrouded in black crepe, is Jim Creighton, who gazes down on the entire scene, as if from heaven. He is the largest of all the figures.

CHAPTER SEVEN

Gentleman's Agreement: The Civil War, Professionalism, and Race

The baseball color line was broken in 1946. That year the Brooklyn Dodgers signed Jackie Robinson, a short-stop from the Negro Leagues, to a contract with one of their Minor League farm clubs. The following season the Dodgers called him up and Robinson became the first African American to play in the Major Leagues since the brief appearances of Moses Walker and Welday Walker with Toledo of the then-Major League American Association in 1884. Jackie Robinson's arrival meant the end of a system that had been one of professional base-ball's oldest and most cherished traditions—on one side of the color line were the Negro Leagues, where African Americans played; and on the other side were the Major and Minor Leagues, which accepted white players only.

The Robinson episode, however, was not the first or the last race-related controversy in the history of baseball. The story of the color line—at least on the playing field—may have ended in the 1940s, but it had a beginning and a middle as well. The color line began when and where baseball began—in the northeastern cities of

New York, Boston, and Philadelphia in the middle decades of the nineteenth century. African Americans were excluded from the first baseball clubs. Later on, they were excluded from the NABBP and the first professional leagues, all of which were based in the Northeast. The great irony in all of this is that in the 1860s the Northern states fought a long, bloody civil war to end the evil of African-American slavery in the South. For twelve years after the war ended, the Union army remained in the South, while the federal government sought to overcome the legacy of slavery and guarantee civil rights for African Americans. The irony was lost, however, on the northerners who controlled baseball. Part of the tragedy of race in American history is that at the very same time that baseball began to promote itself as America's national game—and as the embodiment of American virtues such as fairness, equality, and democracy— baseball was as much a Jim Crow, or segregated, institution as any in the South.

Neither the Knickerbockers nor any of the other pioneer baseball clubs in New York City and Brooklyn admitted a single African-American member during the 1840s and early 1850s. During the 1850s and 1860s, no African-American club was admitted to the NABBP. Since white journalists and baseball writers of the time tended to ignore the African-American community, little is recorded about African-American baseball before the Civil War. But there is no question that African Americans played baseball in New York, Brooklyn, Philadelphia, and Boston. No doubt, some of them played it very well. Scattered mentions in contemporary newspapers refer to exclusively African-American baseball clubs named the Unknowns, Monitors, and Colored Unions— all located in Brooklyn. Philadelphia had several African-American baseball clubs as well. Both cities had relatively prosperous African-American communities with a middle class that could support amateur sporting clubs, just as the white middle class in New York City had supported the Knickerbockers, Gothams, and Eagles. In 1867, after a series of matches between white clubs that were billed as deciding the "championship of the United States," two African-American clubs, the Excelsiors of Philadelphia and the Uniques of Brooklyn, met in a one-game showdown for the "colored championship of the United States." The game was held at the Satellite Grounds, which was located next to the famous Union Grounds in Williamsburg, Brooklyn. A large crowd saw the visiting Excelsiors win by a score of 42-37.

At first, baseball was not openly or officially segregated. Few clubs actually passed written rules excluding African Americans. This is because race was largely a forbidden topic. Like many other all-white institutions of the time in the North and in the South, baseball considered it perfectly acceptable to practice segregation and discrimination—but not to talk about it. Most white baseball clubs used unwritten, so-called gentleman's agreements to exclude African Americans. That way they could continue to claim with a straight face, in the words of Albert Spalding, that "base ball is a democratic game, . . . knowing no arbitrary class distinctions."

The Civil War came along just as baseball was beginning to be regarded as a national, not just a northeastern sport. Baseball lapsed into a kind of suspended animation during the war years of 1861–1865. Only 34 clubs attended the NABBP convention of 1861, down from 62 the year before. In 1862, 32 clubs attended; in 1863, 28; and in 1864, 30.

But the few clubs that remained kept playing, and some of the trends of the prewar years continued. One of those trends was the success of big events like the 1858 Fashion Course series. In the fall of 1861, for instance, ten thousand fans came to the Elysian Fields in Hoboken to watch an all-star team from Brooklyn, led by pitcher Jim Creighton, avenge the defeat of 1858 by beating a team of New York all-stars by a score of 18-6. The match was sponsored by Henry Chadwick and the *New York Clipper*, which provided a silver baseball as a winner's trophy. The idea of the silver ball caught on, and over the next few years "silver ball" or "gold ball" matches were played to determine the club championship of the New York metropolitan area. Newspapers in Boston and other baseball strongholds offered their own silver or gold baseballs to their local champions. Continuing the trend begun by the Excelsiors on their famous tour, more and more clubs traveled long distances to play in other cities. With the addition of ex-Eckford star Al Reach, the Philadelphia Athletics became strong enough to compete on the same level as most New York and Brooklyn clubs. Visiting New York in June of 1865, the Athletics surprised the baseball world by defeating the Eagles, the Unions, and the Gothams.

Two other trends that continued during the war years were the tolerance of faster and faster pitching—what the *New York Times* deplored, in 1863, as "[the] rage for swift pitching"—and the further professionalization and commercialization of the game. The increasing influence of money in baseball was a bigger problem than it might have been because of the NABBP's refusal to acknowledge it. Instead of allowing clubs and players to make a living in an open, aboveboard way, the NABBP rules fostered a situation in which money changed hands in secret. This led to a general atmosphere of hypocrisy that opened baseball up to corruption by gamblers and others who wanted to make a dishonest buck off sports.

In 1865 baseball was rocked by a gambling scandal that marked the beginning of an era of gambling-related corruption that would persist until the arrival of Commissioner Kenesaw Mountain Landis in 1921. On September 28, 1865, the New York Mutuals were scheduled to meet the Brooklyn Eckfords at Elysian

The Philadelphia Athletics of 1865

Fields. Just before the opening pitch, fans' suspicions were aroused by a series of strange fluctuations in the betting odds on the game's outcome. In a short time the odds changed from 100-60, in favor of the Mutuals, to 100-80; by game time the odds were even. The game itself was no less unusual. Leading 5-4 in the fifth, the normally slick-fielding Mutuals gave up eleven runs on an assortment of dropped fly balls, wild throws, and outrageous passed balls by catcher William Wansley. Wansley and two teammates, third baseman Ed Duffy and shortstop Thomas Devyr, were brought up before the NABBP judiciary committee on charges of having thrown the game, presumably on behalf of gamblers. Even though the NABBP expelled Wansley and Duffy, the Mutuals were able to use political influence to have the charges against Devyr dropped. Devyr played shortstop for the Mutuals in 1866; the other two were back in baseball within five years. Run by the supercorrupt William Marcy "Boss" Tweed, the leader of New York City's Tammany Hall political machine, the Mutuals gave off a particularly bad odor. They were, however, only one of many clubs of the 1860s who were suspected of having fixed games or manipulated scores or odds.

Some have claimed that the Civil War may have actually helped spread baseball across the country by mixing soldiers from baseball hotbeds like New York City together with men from other states. This was the view of Albert Spalding. While this may have been motivated largely by wishful thinking—or by the kind of misguided patriotism that gave rise to the Abner Doubleday myth—there are written accounts, drawings and even photographs that tell of wartime baseball matches played among Northern troops in Southern prison camps and in Union campgrounds in the South. On Christmas Day of 1862, a New York unit called Duryea's Zoaves—whose trademark baggy pantaloons were adopted by a number of baseball teams both during and after the Civil War—played a team drawn from the rest of the Union army at Hilton Head, South Carolina. One witness estimated the size of the crowd at forty thousand. This would easily have been the largest baseball crowd in history up to that time. And while it is true that baseball was far from unknown in the South in the prewar years, the level of play there was far below that of the New York and Brooklyn clubs. At events like these, many southerners—white and African-American—saw

A cartoon entitled "When Gambling Controlled"

baseball played for the first time as a serious adult sport. The folk history of the Civil War contains many stories of Southern soldiers playing directly against Northern soldiers, under white flags, during lulls in the fighting.

When the Civil War ended, many soldiers returned home knowing more about baseball than when they had left. Professional baseball stars of the 1870s and 1880s, like National Leaguers Cap Anson from Iowa and Al Spalding from Illinois, remembered learning the game as boys from returning Civil War veterans. Spalding saw baseball as an important unifying force that helped heal the nation's wounds in the postwar and reconstruction years. "It was during the Civil War," Spalding writes in his history of baseball, "that the game of baseball became our national game; for against it there was no prejudice—North or South; and from that day to this it has been played with equal fervor and equal prowess in every section of our beloved country."[1]

When the war ended in 1865, baseball quickly picked up where it had left off. Ninety-one clubs attended the 1865 NABBP convention, and in 1866 the fans across the country followed the exciting national championship series played by the Brooklyn Atlantics and the Philadelphia Athletics. A crowd of more than twenty-five thousand overexcited fans swarmed onto the field and forced the cancellation of game one in Philadelphia. More than fifteen thousand paid to see the rescheduled game at Brooklyn's Capitoline Grounds. All the commotion and excitement caused one newspaper reporter to wonder whether baseball were peaking—a fad that was soon bound to be "played out." NABBP records of 1866 show, however, that the sport was continuing its relentless march west and south. There were now 202 clubs belonging to the NABBP. Although three-quarters of them were located in New York, New Jersey, Pennsylvania, and Connecticut, there were now ten clubs from Washington, D.C.; five from Maryland; two each from Iowa, Tennessee, Mississippi, and Kansas; and one each from Virginia, Kentucky, and Oregon.

The postwar years also saw a concerted effort by the federal government to raise the status of African Americans in the South. Called reconstruction, it represented a commitment to solving the nation's racial problems unparalleled in American history until the civil rights movement of the 1950s and 1960s. The victorious Union army did not go home until 1877, twelve years after General Robert E. Lee's surrender at Appomattox.

It exercised martial law over the South while the federal government attempted to implement a radical program of reform, much of it aimed at improving the status and guaranteeing the civil rights of African Americans. Most African Americans in the South were former slaves, who had been set free by President Abraham Lincoln's Emancipation Proclamation of 1863 and a number of constitutional amendments.

At first, reconstruction inspired great optimism among African Americans everywhere. In 1865 Congress established the Freedmen's Bureau to fund educational programs for African-American ex-slaves and passed the Thirteenth Amendment to the United States Constitution, outlawing slavery everywhere in the country. The following year, Congress passed the Civil Rights Act, which granted full citizenship rights to African Americans. In 1868 it passed the Fourteenth Amendment to the Constitution, when the Civil Rights Act proved insufficient to guarantee citizenship and voting rights to African Americans. This was followed by the Fifteenth Amendment, which required that states not deny or abridge the right to vote on the basis of "race, color or previous condition of servitude."

Those who hoped that the Northern victory in the Civil War and reconstruction might mean a quick end to the color line in baseball were soon to be disappointed. Thanks to a box of long-forgotten documents discovered by the historian Harold Seymour, we now know the inside story of how the African-American Pythian Base Ball Club of Philadelphia tried to join the National Association of Base Ball Players and was rejected because of race. The Pythians belonged to a respectable, middle-class African-American fraternal organization called the Knights of Pythias. The Philadelphia chapter of the Pythians included many prominent leaders of the African-American community. One of these was William Still, who led the fight to integrate Philadelphia's streetcar system in 1866; another was Octavius Catto, a respected soldier, teacher, and athlete whose shooting by a white man in 1871 led to a race riot.

The sad thing about this episode is how similar the Pythians were in every way to their counterparts in white baseball. The Pythian constitution enforced a moral code at least as strict as that of the New York Knickerbockers, requiring that members refrain from gambling, foul language, and hard liquor. Club records show the same devotion to amateurism and lavish hospitality as similar white organizations. After a game against the Mutuals of Washington, D.C., a team of African-American federal employees, the Pythians laid out a spread of wine, assorted meats and cheese, followed up by ice cream and cigars, for their opponents. It is likely that the club played informally against white teams at this time; the Pythians are known to have shared a friendly relationship, as well as playing facilities and umpires, with the famous Athletics. After an official of the Pythians congratulated the Athletics for "upholding the pride of Philadelphia" in an 1868 contest, the Athletics publicly thanked the African-American club for "these manifestations of confidence from our brethren in the city."

None of this friendliness seems to have mattered when the Pythians sent a delegate to apply for membership in the Pennsylvania chapter of the NABBP at that group's 1867 annual convention in Harrisburg. The NABBP's response was a classic example of baseball's historical queasiness and conflicting emotions about issues of race. In the morning of the opening day of the convention, white delegates begged R. S. Bun, the Pythian delegate, to withdraw his application in order to spare the association the embarrassment of having to turn it down for racial reasons; Bun declined. Throughout the afternoon, the officers of the association tried to stall the issue by a series of parliamentary maneuvers.

Each of these, however, was stymied by white delegates who supported the African-American club. In the end, the Pythians and their supporters were able to schedule a formal vote. But when it became apparent at the last minute that the vote would go against the Pythians, a group of white delegates—including some of the same men who had fought for the Pythians' admission—went to Bun and asked him again to give up. In a letter back to his fellow Pythians in Philadelphia, Bun wrote that the association members had treated him very kindly. "[They] seemed disposed," he reported, "to show their sympathy and respect for our club by showing every possible courtesy and kindness." They even paid Bun's train fare home.

This story illustrates the fundamental fact that even though the white baseball establishment—like so many other northern institutions—was wholeheartedly committed to the exclusion of African Americans, it was reluctant to admit that fact openly. It was only when the Pythians made the color line a public issue that the white baseball establishment seemed to suffer a pang or two of conscience over its racist policies. This is shown in the baseball world's guilty reaction to a report that was issued by the NABBP to its members shortly after, and clearly as a result of, the Pythian affair. "It is not presumed by your committee," the report reads, "that any club who have [sic] applied are composed of persons of color, or any portion of them; and the recommendations of your committee are based upon this view, and they unanimously report against the admission of any club which may be composed of one or more colored persons." According to Henry Chadwick, the object of this report was to "keep out of the Convention the discussion of any subject having a political bearing." Elsewhere, Chadwick further offered the rationalization that the report was passed "in the belief that if colored clubs were admitted there would be in all probability some division of feeling, whereas, by excluding them no injury could result to anybody, and the possibility of any rupture being created on political grounds would be avoided"—as though the exclusion of players and clubs because of race was a question of etiquette rather than one of morality.

This report is the only known official NABBP statement on racial exclusion in baseball. After the rejection of the Pythians, African-American baseball players put their efforts into developing their own teams and organizations. In the 1870s and 1880s, new African-American clubs sprang up throughout the East and Midwest and older ones like the Pythians prospered. Octavius Catto's Pythians survived to become a founding member of the League of Colored Baseball Clubs, one of the first African-American leagues, in 1887.

The NABBP-sanctioned color line did not prevent all contact between white and African-American clubs and players. Occasional interracial matches between white and African-American clubs did occur. In September 1869 the Pythians played what was billed as the first formal "mixed" match, against the "City Items," a white team sponsored by the *Philadelphia City Item* newspaper. The Pythians won, 27-17. A couple of weeks later, the Pythians played the Washington Olympics, a national power among white clubs, and lost by 44-23, a score that for that high-scoring era was fairly respectable. During that same fall, another African-American team called the Alerts also issued a challenge to the Olympics. Despite objections from "officious parties" (anti-reconstruction politicians or NABBP officials?), the Olympics accepted, vowing, in General Grant's famous phrase from the Civil War, "to fight it out on this line." In an account drawn from contemporary newspaper coverage, historian Preston D. Orem gives this description of the colorful scene:

> The match drew a large "concourse of friends of
> both" numbering about 5,000, on September

103

20th. The Alerts were nicely uniformed in dark gray shirts, black pants and caps. The Olympics wore their new uniforms of white flannel shirt and pants, a blue cord down the pants leg with buckle just below the knee, light blue stockings, a white skull cap trimmed with blue cord, blue belt, and old English letter "O" on the breast of the shirt. The Alerts looked sharp in practice but collapsed in the game. Olympics, 55; Alerts, 4 (7 innings).[2]

Shortly after this match, the African-American Mutuals, the Pythians' former opponents, made a better showing against the Olympics, losing 24-15.

In spite of the success of interracial events like these, no African-American player or club after the Pythians attempted to cross the baseball color line and join the NABBP. Baseball had moved on to another controversy: the question of how to handle the increasing number of clubs that had been paying their players, thereby breaking NABBP rules on amateurism. The writings of Albert Spalding, however, make it clear that the issue of race remained very much on the minds of the white men in charge of white baseball—and that the issues of race and professionalism may not have been unrelated.

In hindsight, it is clear that from the moment baseball began to change from the small-scale club sport of the 1840s and early 1850s into the regional and national spectator sport of the late 1850s and 1860s, strict amateurism in baseball was doomed. As this change was taking place, while the NABBP continued to pay lip service to the amateur ideal, it took no real action to fight creeping professionalization among its member clubs. In 1860, the NABBP did nothing about rumors that pitcher Jim Creighton was drawing a salary from the Excelsiors. In 1864, Al Reach was accused of accepting one thousand dollars to move from the Eckfords to the Philadelphia Athletics. Two years later, the Athletics were accused of paying three players other than Reach. The NABBP took no action in either case.

By the late 1860s the situation had come to a head. With a great many players on the better teams being paid under the table or through no-show jobs, cheating and double-dealing were rampant. One effect of pretending that the players were not paid was that there was no standard contract or uniform labor-management agreement that regulated player movement. The result was an outbreak of "revolving," or contract jumping, as players traveled from team to team even in mid-season, following the highest bidder. It is a telling commentary on the emptiness of the amateur ideal by 1868 that Henry Chadwick, the chairman of the NABBP rules committee and a man who was regarded as the conscience of baseball, attacked the revolvers for their disloyalty but did not even mention their violation of the amateur ethic. That same year, the NABBP institutionalized its own hypocrisy by setting up a classification system—similar to that of the modern NCAA—which divided NABBP members into an upper and a lower class. Everyone understood that the upper class was, in effect, the pros. This compromise failed to heal the rift in the NABBP between amateurs and professionals. By 1871 the amateurs had split away to form their own organization and the top professional clubs had founded the National Association of *Professional* Base Ball Players, the first modern league.

In his 1911 book, Albert Spalding gives an inside account of the debate over professionalism that took place within baseball during the final days of the old NABBP in 1869 and 1870. As Spalding tells it, there were three main factions. One was the gambling element, which favored the status quo. This is not surprising, since gamblers were able to take advantage of the

Albert Spalding, champion baseball pitcher,
and entrepreneur

weakness of the NABBP and the hypocritical atmosphere prevalent in baseball to bribe players, manipu-
late odds and scores, and even fix the outcomes of
games. Another element was the rank and file membership of the NABBP, who were content to tolerate some
bending of the rules on amateurism but could not com-

pete with the new breed of professional clubs. These clubs correspond to the lower classification in the compromise of 1868. The last of the three elements is described by Spalding as

> that portion of the public—and it was at that time probably in the majority—who believed that baseball was simply an ordinary form of outdoor sport, a pastime, like cricket in England, to be played in times of leisure, and by gentlemen, for exercise, and only incidentally for the entertainment of the public . . . this class felt that the game would suffer by professionalism; that it meant the introduction into the ranks of any man who could play the game skillfully, without regard to his "race, color or previous condition of servitude."[3]

Such a plain reference to race, using the very words of the Fifteenth Amendment, strikes a jarring note with the modern reader. This is partly because Spalding is breaking the taboo against open discussion of race, and partly because there is no pretense here that African Americans could not compete with whites on the baseball field—the standard excuse for excluding African Americans from the Major Leagues in the twentieth century. What Spalding is saying is that a key reason for holding on to the pretense of amateurism in baseball in the 1860s was to justify and preserve the color line. If baseball players became professionals they would be judged solely on performance, not on social standing. And if that were to happen, then how could competent African Americans be kept out?

That question would be partially answered in the 1880s, when the fears of Albert Spalding's "majority of the public" would be realized and dozens of African Americans would cross the baseball color line to play in the white professional leagues.

CHAPTER EIGHT

Big Red Machine: The Wright Brothers and the Red Stockings

When the Wright brothers are mentioned today, most people think of Wilbur and Orville, the men who, in 1903, flew America's first aircraft from a sand dune at Kitty Hawk, North Carolina. To a nineteenth-century baseball fan, however, there was only one pair of Wright brothers—Harry and George. Both Harry and George Wright were baseball players. George was the greatest shortstop—and one of the greatest all-around players—of the 1870s; Harry was a good outfielder, but he became much more famous as the manager of some of the greatest teams in the early days of the professional era in baseball. There was also a lesser-known third baseball-playing Wright brother, Sam. An argument could be made that the baseball Wright brothers were as important to baseball as the flying Wright brothers were to aviation.

The Wrights had two things in common with Henry Chadwick (and a significant number of other prominent figures in early baseball)—they were first- or second-generation English immigrants, and they played cricket.

Harry Wright, baseball's first great manager

Their father, Sam Wright, came to New York from Sheffield, England, in 1836 in order to take a job as cricket pro with the famous St. George Cricket Club. Sam Wright settled down in New York City, not suspecting that he was raising his four sons in what would soon become the cradle of the new sport of baseball. Even though all of them began as cricketers, three of the Wright boys, Harry, George, and Sam, would eventually be bitten by the baseball bug. In many ways, the story of the Wright family is the story of early baseball in microcosm. The Wright brothers moved from cricket to baseball at about the same time that baseball took cricket's place as America's number one sport. Harry Wright was a member of the Knickerbockers, baseball's first club, and as manager of the first openly professional team, was on the cutting edge of the movement to legitimize professionalism in baseball. George Wright was one of the first highly paid professional stars of the 1860s and a notorious "revolver," or player who moves from team to team, in an era when revolving was one of baseball's biggest problems.

Sam Wright, Jr., the youngest Wright brother, was a "good field-no hit" shortstop who played parts of four seasons in the major leagues during the late 1870s. The high point of his career was his appearance with an American baseball team that traveled to England for a series of baseball and cricket matches against the All-England cricket team in 1874; he was chosen for the trip mostly because of his cricket ability.

George Wright, one year older than Sam, was a baseball prodigy. He starred with the New York Gothams in 1864 at the age of sixteen. From then until 1870, he bounced around from one team to another. George Wright was a brilliant fielder, who was credited with being the inventor or—with Atlantics shortstop Dickey Pearce—the coinventor of the modern shortstop position.

George Wright was also a pioneer off the field—a pioneer of professionalism. He was a member of the

110

first generation of Eastern stars to travel West or South, following the highest bidder for his services. This was in the days when NABBP rules strictly prohibited players from accepting any money, so we do not know much about how, or how much, players like Wright were paid. At least on one occasion, his salary appears to have taken the form of a no-show job. In 1867, Wright left the Unions of Morrisania and joined the Washington Nationals, a team made up largely of federal government employees. On the team's official roster for that year, George Wright is listed as a clerk working at "238 Pennsylvania Avenue": 238 Pennsylvania Avenue was not a government office building; it was a public park. There is no way of knowing how many of Wright's teammates also worked "outdoors."

The secret paying of players was rampant in the late 1860s, but it was hardly baseball's biggest problem. The NABBP was deeply divided over the professionalism issue, but this was only part of a tremendous cloud of ill will, venality, and negativism that seemed to hang over the sport. Championship series like the silver and gold ball matches in New York City and Boston lost their luster, as the Atlantics, Mutuals, and Unions of Morrisania bickered over the criteria for determining the championship of New York and similar behavior by the Boston clubs led the New England Association to take back its championship ball and melt it down for scrap. The 1868 Cincinnati city championship was marred by accusations that the Buckeye club had bribed—and even drugged—members of the rival Red Stockings. In 1867 and 1868 the top New York and Brooklyn teams acted in concert to deprive the Philadelphia Athletics of a chance to win the gold ball by trading the championship among themselves and making sure that the Athletics never got the opportunity to win the necessary two games from the current champion. In 1867, for instance, the champion Athletics lost the first game of a two-out-of-three-game series with Philadelphia. They then refused to play the second game, claiming that several of their top players were injured. When the Athletics traveled to Brooklyn and showed for the game anyway, the Atlantics responded by sending out their "muffin nine." After this, the Athletics became the latest team to announce that they would never play the Atlantics again.

The practice of revolving was taken to such extremes that there were some men who played on as many as six teams in three years. Others played for more than one team at a time; this was in clear violation of NABBP rules, which required that a player who left one club wait thirty days, later sixty days, before playing with another. In 1865, while a member of the Philadelphia Olympics, George Wright was discovered to be playing also for the Gothams, under the name of Cohen. A player named John Radcliff deserted the Athletics in mid-season in 1868 when the New York Mutuals offered him one hundred dollars. He returned after Philadelphia topped the Mutuals' offer but then ran out on his contract with the Athletics a second time to join the Cincinnati Red Stockings. Many clubs suffered the same fate as the Irvingtons of Irvington, New Jersey, who developed a first-rate club using local talent, only to lose two-thirds of their starting lineup to better-paying clubs after their winning 1868 season. Disgusted after wholesale losses of their players to clubs that lured them with offers of cash, both the venerable Gothams and the Unions of Morrisania joined the ever-growing numbers of clubs who stopped paying their players, dropped out of the NABBP, or abandoned baseball altogether. By 1870 the list of such clubs included some of the oldest, most respected names in baseball, among them the Knickerbockers, Brooklyn Excelsiors, Eagles, Empires, and Philadelphia Olympics.

A *New York Clipper* editorial from 1869 astutely points out the connection between revolving and far more serious forms of corruption: "If neither the pledged word or written agreement of players can bind them, can we place any faith in their playing? Would they not be just as liable to sell a game as sell a club?" The answer turned out to be yes. Henry Chadwick consistently railed against drunkenness, revolving, and poor sportsmanship, but he recognized that baseball's greatest enemy was the influence of gambling. Writing about a game between the Atlantics and Athletics in early 1867, Chadwick describes the open bookmaking that was going on in the stands:

> Men could be seen pushing along the edge of the crowd, holding hundred dollar bills in their hands, calling out their bets just as the blacklegs do at trotting matches. How men, calling themselves respectable, can openly engage in such gambling business, we cannot say, but certes, dozens did so, who occupy positions in city governments as Judges, Aldermen, Councilmen, etc. Of course, . . . it is not to be wondered at that "Faro" and "Keno" are flourishing institutions, or that base ball in some instances has been brought down to the level of "hippodrome [horse] races," in which it is an understood thing beforehand, that the horse on which the most money has been invested to win, shall be the losing horse.[1]

In 1867 George Wright "revolved" to the Washington Nationals, a club that was about to set out on the first baseball tour of the Midwest. This tour did for baseball in Missouri, Ohio, Indiana, and Illinois what the Excelsiors tour of 1860 did for upstate New York and the Middle Atlantic region. Midwestern baseball was improving fast, but few clubs there could hold their own against a good Eastern team like the Nationals; none of them belonged on the same field as a topflight team like the

Athletics, Atlantics, or Mutuals. Wright and the Nationals demolished nearly all of the "country clubs" they encountered; they beat a St. Louis club 113-26. On their ten-game tour, the Nationals scored a total of 735 runs; they hit 32 home runs. George Wright led the team in home runs with 15 and scored an incredible 92 runs. The only surprise of the tour was the Nationals' defeat by an upstart Forest Cities team from Rockford, Illinois, by a score of 29-23, on July 25. This result looked like less of an upset as time went by. Playing on the Rockford team were future Major League superstars Al Spalding and Ross Barnes; both were seventeen years old and unknown in 1867.

Like the Excelsiors, the Nationals professed strict amateurism and refused to accept a share of any gate receipts. A major difference between the two tours, however, is that the Excelsiors paid their own way; the Nationals' expenses were covered by wealthy "backers," who presumably intended to make their money back— and then some—by betting on the games. This situation partially explains the outburst of bad feeling in Chicago that caused the Nationals' tour to end on a sour note.

The problem began on July 26, the day after the Rockford game, when the Nationals traveled to Chicago to face the Chicago Excelsiors. Because the Excelsiors had recently won the title of "Champions of the West" by defeating Rockford in a Fourth of July tournament, the Nationals' loss to that team inspired great optimism among Chicago fans. Many began to believe that the Excelsiors might have a good chance to win their game against Washington. The *Chicago Times* fanned the flames of regional pride, crowing:

> *When the Nationals shall have lived among us a few days, imbibed pure water from the clear depths of Lake Michigan, breathed the healthy breezes from the prairies, and taken a few*

*lessons in base ball playing, they will begin to
realize how profitable has been their trip to the
Northwest.*[2]

A last-minute avalanche of Chicago money came down
on the Excelsiors to win; the Washington backers who
were traveling with their team eagerly covered the bets.
On the afternoon of the game, ten thousand fans paid
fifty cents admission and crowded into Chicago's Dexter
Park. This time, however, the Nationals were in top
form; they played brilliantly and won by a score of 49-4.
Editorials like the one that appeared in the *Times* seem
to have inspired Wright's team to run up the score.

Chicagoans were outraged and humiliated. Local
newspapers, including the *Chicago Tribune*, charged that
the loss to Rockford had been a setup, a "confidence
game" designed to entice Chicago bettors to bet more
money on the Excelsiors. Now it was the Nationals' turn
to be outraged. Club president Frank Jones demanded
a retraction and sent an open letter to the editor of
Chicago Republican, which reads in part:

> *It is false that we travel around the country for
> gambling purposes; it is false that the game with
> the Rockford Club was "thrown;" . . . and, lastly,
> it is false that noted gamblers accompany our
> club, or that such a class is in any way coun-
> tenanced by the National Club. Our defeat on
> Thursday was as legitimate a one as was our
> victory yesterday, and as great a surprise to us,
> and as much of a disappointment as was that
> of the Excelsiors yesterday to their friends
> in Chicago.*[3]

Henry Chadwick was present at both games, and he
scoffed at any suggestion that the Rockford game had
been thrown. While discussing the controversy in his

1868 book, *The Game of Base Ball,* Chadwick quotes the following joke classified ads that were run by one of the few Chicago newspapers that maintained a sense of humor about the hometown team's defeat:

> *Wanted immediately, at the offices of the* Tribune *and* Republican *newspapers, a base ball club that the Excelsiors can beat, and that will agree not to win or carry off any Chicago money.*
>
> *Anybody who has won any Chicago money in the late base ball match is earnestly requested to return it to the afflicted losers, care of the offices of the* Chicago Tribune *and* Republican.[4]

Club president Jones got the reaction that he asked for, but Chicago's wounded pride was a long time in healing. Ultimately, the Washington Nationals' tour and the affair of July 26 contributed to a growing division in baseball between East and West. Regional tension would soon become a major stimulus toward professionalism in baseball as Western clubs, determined to outdo the Eastern competition, hired more and more star players away from Brooklyn, New York, and Philadelphia. Much later, East-West rivalry would contribute to the formation of the National League, which was based in Chicago (which was then, of course, considered a "Western" city), and the American League, which began as a Western minor circuit. East-West rivalry became part of the structure of the modern Major Leagues when the two leagues were divided into Eastern and Western Divisions in 1969.

George Wright left the Nationals after one year and returned to New York. In the early 1870s, he became the biggest star of baseball's first Major League, the National Association (NA). Playing for the Boston Red Stockings, Wright dominated the shortstop position at a time when pitching was relatively less important, and

Hard-hitting shortstop George Wright

infield defense was relatively more important, than in today's game. Right-handed hitters were known to have batted left-handed against the Red Stockings in order to keep the ball away from Wright, who played bare-handed but, in writer Lee Allen's phrase, "covered his position like a London fog." During Wright's five years with Boston, the Red Stockings won four NA pennants; the year they failed to win, 1871, George Wright was injured and played only sixteen games. He was also the league's best hitter, batting .378—with power—in 1873, and never lower than .336 in any NA season. Wright never mastered the art of hitting the curveball, and his career faded in the late 1870s, as more and more major league pitchers learned how to throw the curve. But his name remained a household word long after his last .300 season. "Who is there," the *New York Clipper* asked in 1880, "who does not know George Wright?"

Harry Wright, the oldest of the baseball-playing Wright brothers, was born in England in 1835. The son of a professional athlete, he had no use for the hypocrisy of the NABBP stance on professionalism. He took a practical approach to money and sports: while he was fiercely honest and as austere in his personal life as Henry Chadwick, Harry Wright saw nothing wrong with making a living from sports. In both English and American cricket, there was no pretense of universal amateurism; players who wished to do so were allowed to work openly as professionals. For years, Wright's athletic life was divided between cricket, which was his job, and baseball, which he played as an amateur.

The two halves of Harry Wright's life came together in 1868 in Cincinnati, Ohio. Wright had been hired by the Union Cricket Club of that city as cricket pro in August of 1865; in his spare time he helped form the Cincinnati Red Stockings baseball club, which elected him captain. The baseball team did reasonably well against local opposition, but the fans of Cincinnati were very disappointed when their team was destroyed by George Wright's Washington Nationals, 53-10, during the Nationals' 1867 tour. In November of that year a group of Cincinnati businessmen led by lawyer and entrepreneur Aaron Champion, decided to improve the Red Stockings. The first thing Champion did was to hire Harry Wright away from the Union Cricket Club; Wright was named player/manager of the Red Stockings at a salary of twelve hundred dollars per year.

Champion went about building a winning team in a very modern, very businesslike way. The Red Stockings were set up like a corporation; they were answerable to a board of directors and they sold stock, raising twenty-six thousand dollars to refurbish their playing field and hire players. Management and labor were distinct and there were clear lines of authority. The most significant difference, however, between Champion's club and every other baseball club in the country was that the Cincinnati players were to be paid openly and above-board. This was in utter defiance of NABBP rules. Like modern ballplayers, they were also to be signed to legally enforceable annual contracts, instead of under the table and by the game, week, or month. There was to be no "revolving" and, ideally, no corruption on the Cincinnati Red Stockings.

In 1868 and 1869, Wright was given a budget and permission to hire as many of the best players in the country as he could. He did not get all of them, but he came close. The 1869 Red Stockings were a virtual national all-star team. Wright signed third baseman Fred Waterman from the Mutuals, pitcher Asa Brainard from the Excelsiors, right fielder Cal McVey from the Actives of Indianapolis, catcher Doug Allison from the Geary club of Philadelphia, and both second baseman Charlie Sweasy and left fielder Andy Leonard from the New Jersey Irvingtons. Dick Hurley was the tenth, or utility, man. George Wright played shortstop; Harry Wright himself played center field. Only first baseman Charlie Gould was a native of Cincinnati. The makeup of the Red Stockings shows that Harry Wright had a keen eye for baseball potential as well as for performance. The nineteen-year-old McVey, one of the few players on the team who was not already a national

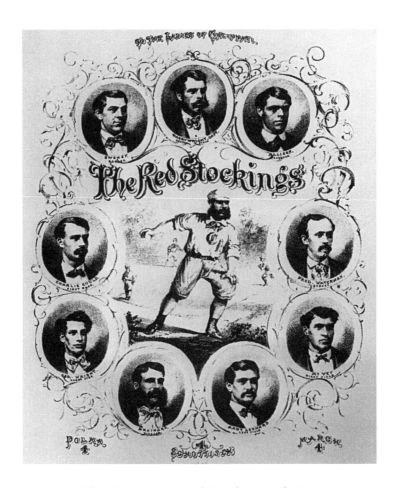

The Cincinnati Red Stockings of 1869
on a sheet music cover

star, developed quickly into an excellent hitter and out-fielder. He went on to hit .362, with terrific power, over five National Association seasons in the 1870s. For the 1869 season, the players were paid a total of $9,300, divided as follows:

George Wright	$1,400
Harry Wright	$1,200

Asa Brainard	$1,100
Fred Waterman	$1,000
Charles Sweasy	$800
Charles Gould	$800
Douglas Allison	$800
Andrew Leonard	$800
Calvin McVey	$800
Richard Hurley	$600

The 1869 Cincinnati Red Stockings were a new kind of baseball team, and Harry Wright wanted them to play a new kind of baseball. Wright ran a tight ship and stressed discipline, teamwork, and total dedication to winning. When one player asked him for permission to miss a few days of practice, Wright replied: "Professional baseball is a business, and as such I trust you will regard it while the season lasts." The Red Stockings practiced hard, worked hard, and played like a well-oiled machine. They backed up bases, hit cutoff men, and thrilled their fans with trick plays that took advantage of the many loopholes that existed in the rules of that time. George Wright and his fellow infielders, for example, were adept at intentionally dropping a fly ball in order to turn a double play when there were men on base and less than two out—this is the play that the modern infield fly rule is designed to prevent. Catcher Doug Allison would sometimes turn an easy 1-4-3 double play by intentionally dropping a third strike with a man on first; under the rules of 1869, this compelled the batter to run to first base, even if that base was already occupied. Harry Wright was the creative genius behind many of the Red Stockings' new tactics. He also outfitted his team in the first baseball uniform to feature the knickers and long socks that players still wear today. The Cincinnati players wore white shirts emblazoned with a large, red letter "C" in Gothic script. By opening day of the 1869 season, Wright's team looked as smart as they played.

The Red Stockings started the season by going unde-feated in a series of games against other Western clubs. On May 31, 1869, Harry Wright's team boarded a train for the start of a monthlong trip to the East. This was the first major tour of the East by a team from the West. The Red Stockings continued their unbeaten streak as they played their way through Cleveland and Buffalo, and across upstate New York to Boston; there they swept the Harvard college team and a strong Lowell club.

The next stop on the tour was New York, where the Red Stockings played and beat their first really first-class opponent, Boss Tweed's New York Mutuals, at Brooklyn's Union Grounds. This game caused a national sensation as one of the most tightly played contests in baseball history. The score was tied, 2-2, when Cincinnati came to bat in the bottom of the ninth. Leadoff man Andy Leonard reached first on an error, but then tried to catch the Mutuals napping by suddenly taking off for second. Leonard was tagged out, but not before getting into a poorly executed rundown—involving all nine of the Mutuals defenders and too many throws to count—that left the crowd in stitches. Leonard's aggressive play seemed to unnerve the Mutuals, who promptly lost the game on a three-base error and a passed ball. Because the rules of the time required the completion of a full nine innings, the Red Stockings finished the inning, adding a fourth run to make the final score 4-2. Even with the addition of the meaningless extra run, this was one of the lowest scores ever in a game between two top clubs. The Red Stockings capped off the trip by sweeping three games from the Atlantics, Eckfords, and Philadelphia Athletics.

When the Red Stockings arrived back in Cincinnati, the streets were lined with flags and team banners. A crowd of four thousand fans, accompanied by a band wearing Zoave-style uniforms, met the players at the railroad station and swept them off to a celebration at the Gibson House hotel, where they feasted on a magnificent banquet that included buffalo tongue *en gêlée,* Westphalian ham à *la Richelieu,* and filet of beef larded with mushrooms and sweetbreads. They were then presented with a gigantic baseball bat of solid wood that measured 27½ feet in length and weighed sixteen hundred pounds. The Red Stockings' names were painted on the barrel. A fan named Carter Gazley then made a speech. "The Eastern papers frequently remarked that you were heavy batters," Gazley said. "If you have any more batting to do, you now have a heavy bat to do it with." Club president Aaron Champion declared that he would rather be president of the Cincinnati Red Stockings than president of the United States.

By midsummer, Harry Wright's juggernaut had become baseball's number one drawing card; the team's growing unbeaten streak had captured the imagination of baseball fans across the country. Everywhere the Red Stockings went, crowds of paying customers came out to see if they could do it again. The closest thing to a Cincinnati loss was a somewhat foul-smelling tie with the Troy Haymakers, also known as the Unions of Lansingburgh, that was played in Cincinnati on August 26. The Haymakers were an unsavory group backed by "Big John" Morrissey, a gambler, bookmaker, and New York City politician who at one time had been heavyweight boxing champion of the world. With the score 17-17 after five innings, Haymakers' president James McKean mysteriously removed his players from the field after a minor argument over a foul tip. This caused a near-riot by the crowd of twelve thousand, and that night, the Cincinnati police had to surround the Haymakers' hotel for their protection. Although the umpire had declared Cincinnati the winner by forfeit, McKean continued to insist that the game was a tie. The reason for all of this became clear when word got out that Morrissey and his friends had bet more than sixty thousand dollars on their team to win. They manufactured the phony tie in order to avoid paying off.

The Red Stockings took advantage of the new rail link with the West Coast to make a tour of California. They returned home still undefeated, after destroying the top clubs in St. Louis, San Francisco, and Nebraska. Wright's team finished the season with wins at home over the Athletics and Mutuals. The 1869 Cincinnati Red Stockings ran up a mind-boggling collection of statistics. They traveled over 11,000 miles by train and played before over 200,000 fans. They outscored their opponents 2,395 to 574; George Wright, the Red Stockings' leading hitter, batted .518, scored 339 runs, and hit 59 home runs in 52 games. In the most important statistic of all, the team played 57 games and won all 57.

Harry Wright and the 1869 Red Stockings did more than win a lot of baseball games. They made professionalism respectable. As Albert Spalding put it, "[They] demonstrated at once and for all time the superiority of an organization of ball players, chosen and trained and paid for the work they were engaged to do, over any and all organizations brought together as amateurs for the simple purpose of playing ball for exercise and entertainment."[5] For this and for his many other contributions to baseball, Harry Wright began to be called, like Henry Chadwick, the "father of baseball." A better title might have been "father of *professional* baseball." When he retired in 1894, Wright was named umpire-in-chief for life of the National League, and the *Sporting Life* wrote of him: "Every magnate in the country is indebted to this man for the establishment of base ball as a business . . . every player is indebted to him for inaugurating an occupation by which he gains a livelihood, and the country at large for adding one more industry (for industry it is in one respect) to furnish employment."[6]

Even before the end of the 1869 season, other clubs were taking a page from Harry Wright's book. In late

July of that year, the New York Mutuals decided to reorganize along the lines of the Cincinnati Red Stockings. They adopted a strict training regimen and introduced a system of fines for missing practice or failing to stay in shape; players who could not adjust to the new rules were dropped. The Mutuals even adopted a new Red Stockings-style uniform: a blue shirt, blue knickers, and long green stockings.

The Cincinnati Red Stockings were still riding their unbeaten streak well into the 1870 season, but it would not be long before they became, like Alexander Cartwright's Knickerbockers, victims of their own success. Harry Wright had shown the way, and the Mutuals and many other clubs followed. Chicago forced the Red Stockings to raise their salaries by hiring its own all-star team and paying them salaries of fifteen hundred dollars each. The competition was getting tougher, and it was only a matter of time before the streak came to an end.

Their lineup essentially unchanged from 1869, on June 14, 1870, the still-unbeaten Cincinnati Red Stockings came to Brooklyn's Capitoline grounds for a game against the Atlantics. The Atlantics were a colorful group that included legendary shortstop Dickey Pearce, defensive whiz Joe "Old Reliable" Start at first base, silent Jack Chapman in left field, Bob "Death to Flying Things" Ferguson behind the plate, and Lipman Pike—major-league baseball's first Jewish player—at second base. A typically rowdy crowd of nine thousand Atlantics fans paid fifty cents, twice the usual admission charge, to see their team attempt to stop the Cincinnati streak at 79-0 games. The Red Stockings played with their usual "clock-like precision" and Atlantics' shortstop Dickey Pearce played brilliantly in the field and on the bases. The score stood at 5-5 at the end of nine innings.

At this point, the Atlantics were perfectly willing to accept a tie; in fact, most of the Brooklyn players had already gone into the clubhouse to change their clothes. But Harry Wright protested that NABBP rules only allowed the games if both captains agreed. Wright wanted to continue. The umpire referred the dispute to Henry Chadwick, the chairman of the NABBP rules committee, who happened to be sitting in the stands. Chadwick ruled that the game should go on.

With Atlantics on first and second and none out in the top of the tenth, George Wright pulled his dropped-ball trick and turned a 5-4 double play. Cincinnati scored two runs in the top of the eleventh, but pitcher Asa Brainard was tiring. Brooklyn got their leadoff man on in the bottom of the inning. With none out, Joe Start drove in the run with a triple to right field past Cal McVey. After Chapman failed to drive in Start with a ground out, Ferguson singled to tie the game. With the crowd in a frenzy, pitcher Zettlein grounded to first baseman Charlie Gould, who threw wildly to the pitcher covering first. As this was happening, Ferguson raced all the way home to win it for Brooklyn by a score of 8-7.

Some observers, including Henry Chadwick, wrote later that they thought Atlantics fans had interfered with McVey while he was trying to field Start's triple. Neither Harry Wright nor any of the other Red Stockings, however, would make excuses. "Atlantics 8, Cincinnati 7. The finest game ever played," Aaron Champion cabled back home to Cincinnati fans. "Our boys did nobly, but fortune was against us. Eleven innings played. Though beaten, not disgraced." The greatest winning streak in the history of baseball was over.

CHAPTER NINE

Major League: The Birth of the National Association

On a rainy St. Patrick's Day evening in 1871, a group of men representing ten of the top baseball clubs in America met at Collier's Rooms, a saloon located at 840 Broadway, a block below Manhattan's Union Square. Nick Young of the Washington Olympics had invited them there for the ostensible purpose of discussing playing schedules for 1871. Everyone knew, however, that the real purpose of the meeting was to plan the destruction of the NABBP and the creation of a new league that would be as openly professional as Harry Wright's 1869 Cincinnati Red Stockings.

Many of the baseball men at the Collier's meeting were apprehensive. After all, by giving up the ideal—or even the pretense—of amateurism, they risked offending many of the fans who supported their clubs by buying tickets to their games. A group of big-name amateur clubs, including the Knickerbockers, Eagles, and Gothams, had already set off in the opposite direction by establishing a truly amateur organization called the National Association of Amateur Base Ball Players.

When Dr. Jones of the Brooklyn Excelsiors wrote a letter to the editor of the *New York Clipper* blaming the professionals for corrupting baseball and for causing all of the problems of the moribund NABBP, he spoke for a significant portion of the baseball community.

Attacks like these, however, only helped convince the professional clubs that they had no choice but to go their own way. The widening split between the professionals and amateurs in the NABBP had become unbridgeable. The point of no return had probably been passed in 1869, with the tremendous success of the Cincinnati Red Stockings. Even though the team fell apart shortly after its dramatic loss to the Atlantics in 1870, by that time a solid majority of the more powerful clubs, and most of the first-rate players, were committed to professionalism. The NABBP tried to save itself by finding a compromise that would allow professionals and amateurs to live under the same roof, but it failed. When a cabal of less than two dozen professional clubs—more or less the same group that attended the St. Patrick's Day meeting—outmaneuvered the amateur majority and took over the NABBP conventions of 1869 and 1870, the amateurs walked out. Before the start of the 1871 season, the NABBP was finished. Few in baseball were sorry. As Albert Spalding wrote,

> *The death of the National Association of Base Ball Players . . . was expected, natural and painless. Everybody who was interested in the welfare of our national game had been looking forward to this consummation, not only with resignation, but with some degree of impatience. The organization had outlived its usefulness; it had fallen into evil ways; it had been in very bad company; and so, when the hour of its dissolution came, no sorrowing friends were there to speak a tearful farewell.*[1]

Before the Collier's meeting ended, the ten teams voted to accept a proposal from a committee led by Harry Wright that they form the National Association of Professional Base Ball Players, or National Association (NA) for short. Admission criteria were simple; a baseball club could join the association by paying a ten-dollar fee. The founding NA clubs were the Philadelphia Athletics, the Troy Haymakers, the Washington Olympics, the New York Mutuals, the Boston Red Stockings, the Rockford Forest Cities, the Cleveland Forest Cities, the Chicago White Stockings, and the Ft. Wayne, Indiana, Kekiongas. The Kekiongas dropped out shortly afterward, and their place was taken by the old Brooklyn Eckfords.

The National Association was the first baseball organization to deserve the title of "Major League." The NA was a departure from the past—and not just because its members openly declared their professionalism. The NA clubs set up a new league structure that was designed to prevent the whole range of problems, including corruption, revolving, and confusion over championships, that had done in the old NABBP. The NA had a strengthened central authority; its president and officers had much more power than those of the NABBP. To avoid the chaos and ill will of the silver and gold ball matches of the late 1860s, the NA spelled out clear criteria for determining the league championship—each NA club was to play a best-three-out-of-five series with every other club, with the winner of the most series being named champion. For the first time, the championship of baseball was called the "pennant."

Unfortunately, in the long run, the National Association proved to be not enough of a departure from the old NABBP. It would collapse after five seasons, undermined by the same corruption and instability that had destroyed its predecessor.

One problem was that the NA did not have strict enough admission standards. Many clubs paid their ten dollars and joined the NA, only to go bankrupt or quit when they found they could not compete; all in all, twenty-five different clubs came and went in the NA's five seasons. The NA did not make an official schedule; it was up to the individual clubs to schedule the required number of series as they saw fit. As a result, it was not at all uncommon for NA clubs who were losing money or who had dropped out of the pennant race to cut costs by skipping a road trip or two. The clubs were also allowed to play an unlimited number of exhibition games before, during and after the NA season; some of them played more games outside the league structure than in it, and fans were often confused about whether or not they were watching a game that would count in the official standings.

Another problem was that the NA central office, while stronger than that of the NABBP, still lacked enough authority to drive out the gamblers who had helped ruin the NABBP. The 1874 NA season was marred by several game-fixing scandals. During a game between the New York Mutuals and the Chicago White Stockings, Mutuals pitcher Bobby Matthews left the game in the fifth inning, complaining of illness. The press and the public, however, suspected Matthews of trying to throw the game—even after the Mutuals produced a note from Matthews's doctor. Also in 1874, the NA unsuccessfully tried to whitewash charges by respected umpire Billy McLean that he had overheard players plotting to fix games. Under tremendous public pressure to take some kind of action, the NA expelled only one of the players. He was reinstated the following season. Throughout the NA's short history, there were dozens, perhaps hundreds, of games that struck fans and sportswriters as "wondrous" or "inexplicable."

The NA proved to be equally inept when it came to combating revolving or resolving disputes over player eligibility. In 1871, for example, Chicago refused to play any games with Troy because of a dispute over the status of former Chicago catcher Bill Craver, who was now playing for the Haymakers. In the Davy Force case of 1875, the NA was unable to stand up to one of its stronger franchises, the Philadelphia Athletics. Force, who played shortstop with Chicago in 1874, had signed 1875 contracts with both Chicago and Philadelphia. When both teams claimed Force's services, the NA central office stepped in and awarded Force to Chicago. Shortly after the election of a Philadelphia ally to the office of NA president, however, the league reversed its own decision and sent Force back to the Athletics. Chicago White Stockings owner William Hulbert was livid. Making an enemy of the powerful and resourceful Hulbert was a mistake that the NA would live to regret.

Finally, as its name implies, the National Association of Professional Base Ball Players was as much an organization of players as of clubs. The financial backers of the NA never had anything like the control over their league that modern baseball owners take for granted. An active player, third baseman Bob Ferguson of the Atlantics, even served as NA president in 1872 and 1873, something that would be unthinkable in any professional sports league today. The players wielded much of the economic power in the NA as well. Boston, the league's most successful franchise, lost $3,000 in 1872 and made about $4,000 in 1873. In those same years it paid its players totals of $16,700 and $14,900 in salary.

The National Association's biggest problem, however, was the Boston Red Stockings. The Red Stockings took more than their name and the color of their socks from the Cincinnati Red Stockings. The team was run by Harry Wright, who had moved to Boston after Cincinnati disbanded in 1870. Wright took with him the nucleus of the powerhouse that had gone 79-0 over two seasons: Cal McVey, now a catcher; first baseman Charlie Gould; and shortstop George Wright. Again,

Harry Wright himself played center field. He also raided the Rockford Forest City club, taking outfielder Fred Cone and two of the young players who had shocked the baseball world by defeating George Wright and the Washington Nationals in 1867: second baseman Ross Barnes and pitching sensation Al Spalding.

Harry Wright's new club was simply too good. They lost a close race to pitcher Dick McBride, second baseman Al Reach, and the rest of the Philadelphia Athletics for the first NA pennant in 1871, but Boston was playing with the severest possible handicap—a serious knee injury to baseball's best player, George Wright. After that, the only suspense for NA fans was waiting to see how many games the Red Stockings would finish ahead of the pack. They went 39-8 in 1872, 43-16 in 1873, and 52-18 in 1874. As time went on, the rest of the league did little to close the gap that separated it from the Red Stockings; in 1875 Boston dominated its opponents to a degree that had not been seen since the 1869 Red Stockings tour. They batted .326 as a team and put together an incredible record of 71-8, fifteen games better than runner-up Philadelphia. The Athletics had nothing to hang their heads about—the last-place Brooklyn Atlantics finished the season 51½ games out. After four years of monotonous Red Stockings victories, even the team's own fans were bored. Attendance in Boston dropped in 1874 and again in 1875.

George Wright was the Babe Ruth of the NA. Wright was a great hitter—he batted .353 in a little over four NA seasons—but it was his fielding at shortstop that made him so valuable. In an era when fielders used their bare hands to stop batted balls and teams made an average of eight or ten errors per game, unearned runs were a huge factor in determining who won and who lost a game. Modern Major League managers often claim that a good shortstop can save his team one or two runs per game over the course of a season, but it does not take

132

much serious consideration to realize that in today's game this is impossible. (Two runs per game, or 324 runs per season, is equivalent, in a normal year, to the entire difference in runs allowed between the top defensive team in the Major Leagues and the bottom; for a single player to make this much of a difference is unthinkable.) The numbers indicate, however, that something approaching this actually may have been true in the case of George Wright. He compiled fielding averages ranging from the high .800s to the low .900s. While these are low by the standards of today, when shortstops commonly field near .980, they are amazing for the 1870s, when many infielders recorded fielding averages in the .700s. The difference between George Wright and an average NA shortstop may have been as much as three errors per game; over the course of a season, three errors per game might well translate into a run or more per game. Wright is the only shortstop in baseball history to achieve a lifetime fielding average over .900 without ever wearing a glove.

George Wright was not the Red Stockings' only weapon, however. They had Ross Barnes and Cal McVey; at .379 and .362, respectively, they were the top hitters in NA history. Barnes was the man who made the "fair-foul" hit famous. The fair-foul hit explains why so many pictures of baseball from the 1870s show the first and third basemen positioned right on the baseline, giving batters an absurd amount of undefended space in the middle of the infield. A fair-foul hit was a ball that the batter intentionally slapped down the baseline so that it bounced in fair territory, crossed either baseline, and then rolled as far as possible into foul territory. By the rules of the time, this was considered a fair ball. A batter with the speed and bat control of a Ross Barnes could easily reach second or even third base on a fair-foul hit.

Harry Wright's team also had the NA's best pitcher, Al Spalding. Spalding threw a fastball with such blazing speed that he sometimes knocked Boston catchers out of the game. He did not throw the curveball, a recent invention that remained a rarity until the second half of the decade. The curveball was discouraged by the fact that NA catchers wore no masks or padding, and by the NA pitching rules, which did not allow a pitcher to throw at an arm angle above dead underhand until 1872. Even after that, a pitch had to be delivered with the hand no higher than hip-level. But Spalding had a devastating "dew drop," or change-up, that kept opposing hitters honest. Spalding dominated NA pitching in a way that no pitcher would ever dominate another Major League. Taking the mound, like most NA pitchers, nearly every day, Spalding won 205 games and lost only 53 over five years. He led the NA in wins in each of its five seasons and led the NA in wins and shutouts four times. In 1872 he went 38-8 and compiled an incredible won-lost record of 55-5 in 1875. Also in 1875, Spalding single-handedly ended the pennant race early by reeling off twenty wins in a row to start the season.

With all of its problems, the formation of the National Association was a step in the right direction for baseball. The future of the sport lay not with a return to the amateurism of the 1850s, but with cleaner, stronger, more disciplined professional leagues. It would be these kinds of leagues that would produce the high-quality, supercompetitive brand of baseball that has given the nation's fans so many great records, thrilling pennant races, and heart-stopping postseason battles—from the first interleague series of the 1880s, to the golden seasons of the 1920s and 1930s, to the great divisional races, playoff games, and World Series of the 1980s and 1990s.

As baseball's first experiment with the idea of a professional league, the National Association may not have worked well enough to last, but it worked well enough to be tried again. As for the Knickerbockers and the other clubs that were trying to turn back the clock to the days before baseball became an "industry," they were doomed to failure. The amateur national association that they formed in 1871 disbanded within a year. Some of the old baseball clubs from the 1840s and 1850s, like the Knickerbockers, continued for a little while longer to play informally among themselves. Others took up yachting or other safely amateur sports; the Brooklyn Excelsiors abandoned sports altogether and evolved into one of New York City's most exclusive men's social clubs, lasting well into the twentieth century. At around the same time that baseball formed the National Association, committing itself to the path of professionalism, John C. Stevens's baseball grounds in Hoboken, for decades the center of amateur baseball, fell out of use. From then on, baseball would be played behind walls in ballparks shoehorned into city blocks, as near as possible to the tens of thousands of fans whose hard-earned money gave the owners their profits and paid the players their salaries. Baseball would never return to the Elysian Fields.

SOURCE NOTES

CHAPTER ONE
1. Irving Leitner, *Baseball: Diamond in the Rough* (New York: Criterion Books, 1972), p. 31.
2. Ibid., p. 33.

CHAPTER TWO
1. Robert Henderson, *Bat, Ball and Bishop* (New York: Rockport Press: 1947), p. 189.
2. Henry Chadwick, *The Game of Base Ball* (New York: George Munro and Co., 1868), p. 9.

CHAPTER THREE
1. Charles Einstein, ed., *The Third Fireside Book of Baseball* (New York: Simon and Schuster, 1968), p. 129.
2. Preston D. Orem, *Baseball (1845–1881), from the Newspaper Accounts* (Altadena, Calif.: Self-published, 1961), p. 11
3. Harold Seymour, *Baseball, the Early Years* (New York: Oxford University Press, 1960), p. 20.
4. Orem, *Baseball (1845–1881)*, pp. 4–5.

5. Ibid., p. 13.
6. Ibid., p. 24.
7. John Thorn and Pete Palmer, eds., *Total Baseball, Third Ed.* (New York: HarperCollins, 1993), p. 6.

CHAPTER FOUR
1. Preston D. Orem, *Baseball (1845–1881) from the Newspaper Accounts* (Altadena, Calif.: Self-published, 1961), pp. 4–5.
2. Irving Leitner, *Baseball: Diamond in the Rough* (New York: Criterion Books, 1972), p. 48.
3. George B. Kirsch, *The Creation of American Team Sports* (Urbana and Chicago: University of Illinois Press, 1989), p. 55.

CHAPTER FIVE
1. George B. Kirsch, *The Creation of American Team Sports* (Urbana and Chicago: University of Illinois Press, 1989), p. 30.
2. Ibid., p. 36.
3. Henry Chadwick, *The Game of Base Ball* (New York: George Munro and Co., 1868), p. 10.
4. Irving Leitner, *Baseball: Diamond in the Rough* (New York: Criterion Books, 1972), p. 119.

CHAPTER SIX
1. George B. Kirsch, *The Creation of American Team Sports* (Urbana and Chicago: University of Illinois Press, 1989), p. 189.
2. Harold Seymour, *Baseball, the Early Years* (New York: Oxford University Press, 1960), p. 25.
3. Albert Spalding, *America's National Game, rev. and ed. by Samm Coombs and Bob West* (San Francisco: Halo Books, 1991), p. 51.
4. SABR: *19th-century Stars* (1989), p. 32.
5. Spalding, *America's National Game*, p. 63.
6. Ibid., p. 59.

CHAPTER SEVEN

1. Albert Spalding, *America's National Game*, rev. and ed. by Samm Coombs and Bob West (San Francisco: Halo Books, 1991), p. 65.
2. Preston D. Orem, *Baseball (1845–1881) from the Newspaper Accounts* (Altadena, California: Self-published: 1961), p. 99.
3. Spalding, *America's National Game*, pp. 82–83.

CHAPTER EIGHT

1. Henry Chadwick, *The Game of Base Ball* (New York: George Munro and Co., 1868), p. 142.
2. Ibid., p. 94.
3. Ibid., pp. 104–105.
4. Ibid., p. 107.
5. Albert Spalding, *America's National Game*, rev. and ed. by Samm Coombs and Bob West (San Francisco: Halo Books, 1991), pp. 84–85.
6. Harold Seymour, *Baseball, the Early Years* (New York: Oxford University Press, 1960), p. 25.

CHAPTER NINE

1. Albert Spalding, *America's National Game*, rev. and ed. by Samm Coombs and Bob West (San Francisco: Halo Books, 1991), p. 93.

ℬIBLIOGRAPHY

Alexander, Charles. *Our Game.* New York: Henry Holt and Co., 1991.

Allen, Lee. *100 Years of Baseball.* New York: Bartholomew House, 1950.

———. *Hot Stove League.* New York: A.S. Barnes and Co., 1955.

Asbury, Herbert. *Ye Olde Fire Laddies.* New York: Alfred A. Knopf, 1930.

Benson, Michael. *Ballparks of North America.* Jefferson, N.C.: McFarland and Co., 1989.

Carter, Craig, ed. *Daguerreotypes*, 8th ed. Saint Louis: Sporting News, 1990.

Chadwick, Henry. *The Game of Base Ball.* New York: George Munro, 1868.

Goldstein, Warren. *Playing for Keeps, A History of Early Baseball.* Ithaca: Cornell University Press, 1989.

Henderson, Robert. *Bat, Ball and Bishop.* New York: Rockport Press, 1947.

James, Bill. *The Bill James Historical Baseball Abstract.* New York: Villard Books, 1988.

Kirsch, George. *The Creation of American Team Sports.* Urbana: University of Illinois Press, 1989.

Leitner, Irving. *Baseball, Diamond in the Rough.* New York: Criterion Books, 1972.

Orem, Preston D. *Baseball (1845–1881) from the Newspaper Accounts.* Altadena, Calif.: Self-published, 1961.

Rucker, Mark. *Base Ball Cartes, The First Baseball Cards.* Saratoga Springs, N.Y.: Self-published, 1988.

Ryczek, William. *Blackguards and Red Stockings, A History of Baseball's National Association, 1871–1875.* Jefferson, N.C.: McFarland and Co., 1992.

Seymour, Harold. *Baseball: The People's Game.* New York: Oxford University Press, 1990.

———. Baseball: *The Early Years.* New York: Oxford University Press, 1960.

Spalding, Albert. *Base Ball, America's National Game.* Rev. and ed. by Samm Coombs and Bob West. San Francisco: Halo Books, 1991.

Thorn, John, and Palmer, Pete, eds. *Total Baseball,* 3rd ed. New York: HarperCollins, 1993.

Tygiel, Jules. *Baseball's Great Experiment.* New York: Oxford University Press, 1983.

Zoss, Joel, and Bowman, John: *Diamonds in the Rough.* New York: Macmillan, 1989.

INDEX